30p

I. L. Baker BA

Brodie's Notes on Thomas Hardy's

Jude the Obscure

I0854411

Pan Educational London and Sydney

First published 1977 by Pan Books Ltd
Cavaye Place, London, SW10 9PG
1 2 3 4 5 6 7 8 9
© I. L. Baker 1977
ISBN 0 330 50062 7
Printed and bound in Great Britain by
Richard Clay (The Chaucer Press) Ltd, Bungay, Suffolk

Contents

To the student 1

The author 3

Critical comment 9
General 9
Unique features 10

Major themes 14
Marriage 14
Education 18
Religion and nature 23
Sexuality 28

Structure 31

Style 35

Characters 41

Chapter summaries and textual notes 66

Revision questions 119

General questions 123

Page references in these Notes are to the Macmillan
New Wessex edition of *Jude the Obscure*, but references are
usually given to particular parts and chapters, so that
the Notes may be used with any edition of the book

To the student

1 The student must remember that the Hardy text is his first and closest priority, and that these Notes are in no way intended as a substitute for, but only as a complement to, the novel itself.

2 It would be unwise for the student, faced with a novel of some length and complexity, to read at this stage too much of what has been written about Hardy, around whom an enormous literature has grown. Some guidance may therefore be acceptable.

Biographical works (the name is abbreviated throughout).
The Life of T.H. 1840–1928: Macmillan, 1962. This standard biography, nominally by Hardy's second wife, was in fact prepared by Hardy himself: it is indispensable, despite its omissions and discreet silences. In these Notes all quotations not otherwise ascribed are taken from this book.
Young T.H., R. Gittings (Heinemann, 1975)
T.H., Edmund Blunden (Macmillan, 1941)
T.H., E. Hardy (Hogarth Press, 1954)
T.H., D. Brown (Longmans, Green & Co, 1954)

Apart from those books containing some critical treatment specifically on *Jude*, the student is advised to limit his attention to particular points (of character, style, and so on) by a discriminating use of the indexes of the following books. There is no point in attempting to read through all these in earnest detail.

H. The Novelist, Lord David Cecil (Constable, 1943)
T.H., Harold Child (Nisbet, revised 1925)
T.H., The Novels and Stories, A. J. Guerard (OUP, 1949)
Eight Modern Writers, J. I. M. Stewart (OUP, 1963)

Hardy, George Wing (Oliver & Boyd, 1963)
The Genius of T.H., edited by M. Drabble (Weidenfeld & Nicolson, 1976)

A sound overall guide to Hardy studies is to be found in *A Hardy Companion* by F. B. Pinion (Macmillan, 1968)

The author

Thomas Hardy was born on 2 June 1840, in a brick and thatch house in the hamlet of Upper Bockhampton, in the parish of Stinsford, near Dorchester, in the English county of Dorset. Here his father was born and died, and here, or close by, Hardy himself spent the major part of his life. The father, a buoyant and kindly man, was a master-mason (or builder); quite well-to-do but unambitious, and devoted to music – for Hardys had played and sung the music for the Stinsford Parish Church for over a hundred years. This passionate interest in music Hardy inherited: he could tune a fiddle as a lad, play it as a youth at weddings and festivals; and he would join in the dancing, often weeping with emotion. We know that, all his life, he was extremely sensitive to music, and he long remembered the tunes of his childhood. His mother (and her mother too) was an omnivorous reader, and cast in a heroic mould. 'She was of the stuff of which great men's mothers are made' is said of a character in his powerful novel *Far From The Madding Crowd*; but it could well have applied to, and might even have been a recollection of, his own mother.

Hardy was a delicate child (he had to be resuscitated at birth) and had no formal schooling until he was eight: but his mental precocity, the atmosphere of books and music, and the rich well-watered countryside around sufficiently fed his imagination. Besides, like his father, he was completely un-ambitious and had no wish to grow up. This is reflected a little in Part 1, Chapter 2, where the little Jude, the 'natural boy', 'did not want to be a man'. Eventually the village school claimed him, and his reading extended to such material as Dryden's *Virgil* and Johnson's *Rasselas* before he entered the Dorchester day-school, where at fourteen he won a prize for diligence. He had started Latin at the age of twelve (again, like Jude), then read his Virgil in the original: he also devoured the works of Shakespeare, Scott, Dumas, Milton and sundry popular novelists of the day. He had extra lessons in French and German, and taught at Sunday School, learning the services and much of the Bible by heart. Hardy was popular at school: yet he remained essentially aloof, a lover of solitude. He was fastidious, could never bear anyone touching him. And he had already – through his classical reading, his observation of life around him in an era of painful change and the sight of some public hangings – gained a stark view of the injustices and tragedy of human life.

At the age of twenty, Hardy went into the offices of an ecclesiastical architect in Dorchester: his master, John Hicks, was an educated man and a competent classical scholar. Hardy usually rose early to study his Latin (often at 4 a.m. in the summer), and learned Greek on his own: his already marked intellectual precocity flourished and blossomed with contacts such as his master, a near-neighbour William Barnes (a dialect poet and philosopher), other scholarly acquaintances and fine craftsmen. A year later he was in London, still working as an architect and restorer, but widening his reading and artistic bent in the cultural wealth of the capital. He visited its museums, galleries and libraries: he studied painting especially, being particularly interested in light and shade effects. He read deeply and widely in all manner of subjects, particularly in science and philosophy. The works of Darwin, Huxley, J. S. Mill and Herbert Spencer, whose unorthodoxy in various fields had an immense influence in liberating thought from traditionally-accepted beliefs, had a profound effect on the young Hardy (and there are constant references and echoes throughout our novel): by the age of thirty he was intellectually an agnostic. More practically, however, he had to decide, despite his inherent lack of ambition, what to do for his adult livelihood. He considered art-criticism, even the Church, play-writing, and architecture, for which he had been long trained and at which he was undoubtedly competent. He made his way back to Dorchester, still professionally an architect, but finding time to write some occasional verse, and then a novel, *The Poor Man and the Lady*, which the publishing house of Macmillan rejected. In 1871, another attempt, *Desperate Remedies*, appeared: this he paid a lesser-known firm to publish. The book made little impact, yet despite its experimental nature it bears what we now recognize as the Hardy stamp; with its rather morbid episodes, its church and churchyard scenes, a certain air of fantasy, and some emotional force. All these elements were intensified and improved in his next novels: *Under The Greenwood Tree*, an idyll of the Wessex scene; and *A Pair of Blue Eyes* (1873), much more skilful and ambitious. During this time Hardy met Emma Gifford on one of his church-restoration tours. Emma was a devotedly religious, rather solitary, yet vital and graceful woman: they married in September 1874, on the strength of Hardy's next novel, *Far From the Madding Crowd*. This appeared in the illustrious *Cornhill* magazine from January to November 1874, an immediate success both as a serial and as a complete volume. His new wife encouraged Hardy to stick to writing, which he did – caring little for the fame, the wealth, the social success and some hostility which came his way as a consequence.

Therefore, until the age of fifty-eight, Hardy wrote a further ten novels, some short stories and essays, and a play. During this period, and after having moved about here and abroad, he finally settled down at Dorchester in a house of his own design, which he called Max Gate. He had achieved fame and security; his circle of eminent friends had widened enormously. The novels, many pitiless and tragic in theme, often shocked 'Victorian' sentiments and taste. Hardy made few concessions to public opinion, exposing relentlessly his view of the tragic, insoluble problems of human existence for which religion seemed to offer no solution. This negative resigned attitude disturbed many: the reception of *Jude the Obscure* was particularly bitter and hostile (see Notes on the Postscript).

In 1898, Hardy abruptly turned his back on the novel, utterly and completely: he returned to poetry – his first and strongest love – with his collection of *Wessex Poems*. Personal domestic tragedy clouded his life at this period: disharmony had long been growing between Hardy and his first wife. The marriage had been childless, much to his sorrow; religious differences had become more sensitively acute; and Hardy's complete lack of social ambition was a further cause of friction between them. All these factors seem to have culminated in distressing emotional disturbance for his wife, with a tendency towards delusions which, apparently, led to her death. Hardy, in some poignant verse, showed that he felt partly responsible. Two years later, in 1914, he married an old friend of the family, Forence Dugdale, who had been his secretary and was herself a writer. Florence (who later brought out an excellent biography of her husband), by her humour, sympathy and intelligent understanding and criticism of his work, made happy his remaining years.

Sensitive lyrical poetry, of exquisite concentration, craftsmanship and feeling now flowed: the greatest living novelist was hailed as a significant poet; and some critics believe that posterity will rate Hardy even higher as a poet than as a novelist. Honours were showered on this quiet yet sprightly, charming and vigorously intellectual man, especially after the publication of *The Dynasts*, a verse-drama of the Napoleonic Wars and a unique philosophic history and epic drama. Five universities (Scots and English) conferred honorary degrees on one whose formal tuition had never gone beyond Grammar School. He received the Order of Merit in 1910, and the Gold Medal of the Royal Society of Literature in 1911; but his greatest pleasure came from his award of the Freedom of the Borough of Dorchester. His works were constantly reprinted, and he left a fortune of nearly £100,000. He died on 11 January 1928.

The irony which pervades much of Hardy's work was given a dramatic and superb twist after his death. It was decided that the man who have never sought fame should be buried in Westminster Abbey: there were quarrels over precedence for tickets, and the Prime Minister was among the illustrious who bore the pall. The avowed agnostic was buried in England's national shrine. The body was cremated and the ashes interred in Poets' Corner, next to Dickens's grave, with a spadeful of Dorset earth thrown over. But his heart was carried back to Stinsford, and was buried in the grave of his first wife, in the churchyard there.

Critical comment

General

Jude the Obscure is a long book of fifty-three chapters, and involves eight significant characters: there are at least twenty-six references to places, nearly fifty allusions to the Bible, and over forty to other writers and works. It deals forcibly, often critically and sometimes bitterly, with a variety of themes: among these are sex, marriage, fate, historical change, nature, society, institutions, religion, heredity – and tries to place and understand man in his universe. The novel, ever since its bowdlerized serial publication (December 1894 to November 1895), and still more after its appearance in book form, has given rise to a detailed and lengthy scholarly debate, which still continues. The book is praised and condemned with equal force and fervour, and interpreted in widely varying ways and from opposing viewpoints.

These Notes, therefore, must be highly selective, and cannot replace the mass of detail to be found in scores of books on Hardy's life, times and background, or on his style, intentions, structures, etc. Nor can the Notes replace the attentive reader's own feelings and critical consideration. Not every reference or allusion is traced or is even always traceable, but notes are provided wherever significant for an understanding of the text. Far more important than tracking down an obscure Berkshire hamlet or Biblical reference, a minor writer or a passing quotation, is a clear understanding of the underlying themes, and of Hardy's approach to, and intentions about, them and his characters. This further underlines the need for a careful and thorough reading and re-reading of the text; after which, these Notes will (it is hoped) suggest lines of thought to help the attentive reader more fully to appreciate the novelty, richness and power of the total work.

Unique features

There is sharp disagreement as to which of Hardy's novels is his finest achievement: the dispute generally rages around *Jude the Obscure*, *The Return of the Native*, and *Tess of the D'Urbervilles*. But it is certain that *Jude* is in many respects unique.

Firstly, it aroused the most hostile and adverse criticism, which rose to a storm of violent controversy. Mrs Hardy was horrified, and strove to prevent its publication in book form; and the newspapers and literary periodicals (not all: *The Daily Telegraph*, pronounced it a masterpiece) were often violent and scathing. Sue Bridehead was hysterical and abnormal; the book left a nasty taste in the mouth; the novel said a great many insulting things on topics which most people held sacred. Hardy was called 'The Degenerate': he was 'speculating in smut'. *Punch* parodied *Dude the Diffuse*, by Toomuch Too Hardy: and Mrs Oliphant called it 'coarsely indecent'. The *Pall Mall Gazette* summed up: *Jude the Obscene*, a 'mass of filth from beginning to end'. Other similar epithets flowed freely, in a typically Victorian state of high moral indignation: it was disgusting, sordid, a novel of lubricity, a 'studied satyriasis of senility' (Hardy, at the time, was fifty-five!). Now this reaction is significant. It reveals *Jude*, in the history of the novel, as a landmark in time, thought and feeling: it illustrates the distance that society and the scope of the novel have moved. It is Hardy's only novel about his own time: it lies between the complacent optimism of much of the nineteenth century, especially among the genteel and well-to-do, and the prevailing uncertainty and greater gloom of the twentieth. It looks back in part to the romantic idealism of earlier days – for Jude, with his passionate nature and high hopes, is a romantic in part – and yet forward to the greater restlessness of our own times, in our realization that so many problems remain unsolved and perhaps insoluble.

Secondly, of all Hardy's fifteen novels, *Jude* is the one most charged with challenging ideas, perhaps too many of them to be contained in one attempt. Nature, time, marriage, society, education, religion, heredity, the human condition: this multiplicity and complex diversity of ideas nearly damages the integrity of the novel. Some of these topics will be considered separately.

Thirdly, Hardy has lifted *Jude* out of the comfortable and comforting 'Wessex' atmosphere of almost all his previous work. Here there is no background of nature; of natural processes; of historic traditions; of pastoral charm or eternal strengths such as Egdon Heath in *The Return of the Native*, which seemed to cushion man's struggles with inexorable fate and afforded him some retreat from life's bitter ironies. There is no close and cosy community sense: what there is of Wessex (and most places of the novel are in Berkshire) is barren. Gone are the 'rustics' whose rough and bawdy humour could refresh and delight, setting the folly of men and the rigours of blind fate in some perspective. Deliberately, Hardy has restricted his scope, so that everything narrows down to a central outcry of human agony: nothing seems stable. There are no great heroic scenes, no poetry of landscape, no spectacle of the grandeur of natural light and colour, and little richly evocative language. This has the effect of concentrating the impact and power of the novel upon a series of snapshot-like moments, mostly of gloom, frustration, despair, and one of horror.

Next, there is little humour, and that little is wry and ironic. Most of the humour derives from Arabella, who is perhaps in many ways the most odious woman Hardy ever portrayed. There is no lasting joy, little pure laughter. Who laughs in sheer merriment? Who smiles without sadness? Sue and Jude seemed to enjoy the Wessex Agricultural Show (Part 5, Chapter 5); but note Hardy's opening sentence. They are living together, and have had children, but nothing is made of this in terms of domestic bliss: the children are not even named. The note of humourless gloom is struck at the very beginning, with the little Jude suffering for his kindness to the birds, losing his schoolmaster friend, and finding his environment ugly.

Then, there is a pervasive atmosphere of rootlessness and restlessness, also maintained from the start. The very Part Titles – bare names of places – set the tone. There is endless movement: walking, coach and train travel, toing-and-froing of notes and letters, all suggesting strongly the modern age. In his earlier 'Wessex' novels – always set well in the past before his own time – Hardy's villagers, however old, had scarcely left the bounds of their own hamlet or village. Some others, of a higher status, like Eustacia Vye in *The Return of the Native*, yearn to escape; but the 'native' of the novel, Clym Yeobright, rich and successful abroad, returns to stay, and to work as a day-labourer and local lay-preacher. 'Physician' Vilbert, by profession, travels about: but there is an overall sense of people being uprooted, wandering off (like Jude and Sue's own parents): Arabella and her family emigrate, and then return. Phillotson moves from, and eventually – after several changes – returns to Marygreen. Jude and Sue seem to travel about with nowhere to rest their heads. Little Father Time enters the story (magnificently) by a long train-journey and a lonely walk. There is a sense of nervous insta-bility: people are driven on by ambition, hope, or the cruelties of man or fate. And yet most of them seem trapped, often in labyrinths of their own making. It is an unfriendly, be-wildering, malevolent, unstable and indefinite world, in which isolated humans drift, shuttle-like, buffeted and unresting and often tormented. It is a world very much afflicted with what Hardy himself called 'the strange disease of modern life': and very much, one fears, a world we all recognize as ours: fast losing much of its traditional stability, its codes of honesty, tolerance and unselfish human kindness – a fractured world that often seems to have lost its bearings.

In these ways, then, *Jude the Obscure* reads as a watershed, as a point of division in time. Its various themes deal with the failures of an outworn past of old ideas, old systems, old ways of thought: and it gropes forward (not always successfully) towards a newer perspective, newer concepts and fresher values. Jude, on his deathbed, haunted and taunted by dreams, feels that some progress is inevitable: Arabella brings us down to earth with the certainty that many battles between the flesh and the spirit, between the letter and the spirit, have yet to be fought and won. Even now, many of the attitudes that kept Jude obscure and rendered so many of his relationships tragic, have still to change – before humankind is brought to an understanding of all its responsibilities, and finds an effective means of dealing with them.

Major themes

Marriage

The theme of marriage as a social institution (or more strictly, that of divorce) helps to define the principal characters. We know that Hardy (whose first marriage was difficult, childless, and increasingly unhappy) had unconventional views on this as on many other topics. He thought that the legal and religious restrictions making marriage well-nigh indissoluble at that time (for most people, especially the poor), could and did have dreadful consequences and cause great personal bitterness. It could be a trap: '. . . marriage should not thwart nature,' he wrote, and that 'when it does thwart nature it is no real marriage, and the legal contract should therefore be as speedily cancelled as possible. Half the misery of human life would I think disappear if this were made easy . . .'

A great deal of the novel, then, exposes the anomalies of the marriage laws, especially where incompatibility is obvious: in places it jeers and rails cynically at Anglican respectability. It was this aspect (among others) that so horrified Mrs Hardy and many early critics: it appeared an assault on the stronghold of marriage. Hardy remained adamant. In a letter to a friend he said: 'Never retreat. Never explain. Get it done and let them howl.' In an article on the topic, Hardy expressed the view that we lived in 'a barbarous age, and are the slaves of gross superstition'. And again: 'I can only suppose, in a general way, that a marriage should be dissolvable on the wish of either party, if that party can prove a cruelty to him or her, provided (probably) that the maintenance of the children (if any) should be borne by the breadwinner.'

However, it must be realized that here the marriage question is not the central theme; and the divorces of Jude and Sue get through with little fuss or difficulty. The real trouble is

the effects of the absence of marriage, and the marriage ceremony itself. However unorthodox and provoking Hardy's
views are, what is more significant is how he uses them to
establish his characters, colouring their view of society, show-
ing how that society affects them and their children: what
emerges is a moral judgement and an insight into man's
proper relationship with his fellows. Hardy's bitter views are
threaded through the novel. Almost at the beginning (Part 1,
Chapter 2) Drusilla Fawley hints broadly at a marriage 'curse'
on the Fawleys – 'don't *you* ever marry'. Then Arabella Donn
'catches' him, literally with a pig's pizzle, and sensuously by
her ample charms and wiles (Part 1, Chapters 6–9): the last
paragraph of Part 1, Chapter 9 is particularly significant: 'a
gin which would cripple him' is an image that will recur
poignantly. He is again warned by Drusilla in Part 2, Chapter 2, and the penultimate paragraph (pp.109–10) is ominous;
and Drusilla's (and others') reminiscences in Part 2, Chapter 6
accentuate the dangers. A great deal of Part 3 is concerned
with Sue's involvement with Phillotson, and Jude's reactions
to her marriage: the whole section is riddled with wry and
bitter comment (often coloured, of course, by Sue's own
'epicene' viewpoint) on society's inconsistent standards; the
end of Chapter 6 of Part 3 is particularly noteworthy here.
Again, one notices sharp turns of phrase, as when Jude says
to the newly-married Sue that 'Wifedom has not yet squashed
up and digested you in its vast maw as an atom which has
no further individuality' (Part 3, Chapter 9).
  At Shaston (Part 4), too, there are some bitter reflections
on the 'letter and the spirit' of sanctified, legalized union:
Sue is talking of love, which some people can't give 'con-
tinuously to the chamber-officer appointed by the bishop's
licence to receive it.' (p.225). There follows the whole encounter in Part 4, Chapter 2, which culminates in the
repeated symbol of the gin-trap and the snared rabbit. This
is a powerful image, which deserves attention. The rabbit

literally, and the humans who share its agony, metaphorically, are caught in a trap, and are savagely, unnaturally wounded: for none is there escape; for all there must be pain and long-drawn out suffering. And Jude knows the only solution – death. The consequent conversation of the two cousins is poignant and ominous. In Part 4, Chapter 3 Phillotson and his disaffected wife talk of 'Domestic laws' and 'laws and ordinances', and Sue quotes Mill on personal freedom. Poor wretched Phillotson: one must sympathize with his bewildered retort, 'What do I care about J. S. Mill! I only want to lead a quiet life!' (p.244). But in the following chapter (4), while talking to his friend Gillingham, Phillotson comes near to understanding something of his wife's apparent eccentricity. Shaston, in many ways, wipes the slate clean; but then there recurs Sue's instinctive revulsion from the 'letter' of the marriage laws: 'contracted to cherish me under a Government stamp ... licensed to be loved on the premises'. The entire conversation is an analysis of their contrasting positions (Part 5, Chapter 1).

Arabella, of course, has her own earthy, practical views: they are clearly expressed at the end of the next chapter (2). The arrival of her letter about Jude's and her child, Little Father Time, prompts the pair to try again, for the sake of the child, to establish a conventional marriage, and the whole of Chapter 4 of Part 5 deserves careful attention. The doleful tale of Widow Edlin and the foreboding of little Time colour their prospects; and the actuality of the scene at the Registry Office is harsh, bitter, ironic. The day is unpleasant, the place is dreary, the floor is bare and muddy: and note the details of the couple being married – the soldier reluctant, his bride pregnant and battered. The next pair are worse: the man ugly, the woman coarse: he is a gaol-bird; and both are inflamed with drink and 'the satisfaction of being on the brink of a gratified desire'. And the church ceremony elsewhere was an 'object-lesson', a 'business contract' which neither relishes. No wonder the Widow Edlin is amazed: all this is 'new notions'. For her and her husband, marriage was no more to be thought about than a child's game. Hardy does not let up: when Arabella and her husband arrive at the Wessex Show, they soon bicker (he at the bar, flirting; she having purchased a love-philtre from Vilbert) and they leave the beer tent together, 'this pot-bellied man and florid woman, in the antipatheitc, recriminatory mood of the average husband and wife of Christendom' (p.315). The very fact that Jude and Sue look happy is a confirmation for Arabella that they cannot be married.

But Chapter 6 highlights their problems: they and the child suffer the ostracism of their nominally 'Christian' neighbours and become shifting, rootless drifters. In the final Part, the theme runs down into its painful horrors. Again, Hardy maintains his bitterness: against a background of church bells Sue is refused lodging because her pregnancy shows, denied another because there are children, and in the third are accepted only for the night. After the tragedy of the children's deaths, follows a kind of living death for the converted Sue in her re-marriage to Phillotson, and the parody, almost what one would now call a 'black comedy' of Jude's second entrapment by Arabella. Only because their landlord hears them quarrelling, and her flinging things at her husband's head, does he conclude, recognizing 'the note of genuine wedlock', that they must be 'respectable' – not living in sin, that is – a telling irony.

This theme is but one of many: it is secondary to others, such as Hardy's views on religion and education. And one problem allied to it – but far more important in itself in the novel – is the theme of sexual relationships (considered mainly under *Characters*). It is nevertheless essential to bear this perspective in mind: it is part of Hardy's prophetic view of what he called the 'ache of modernism', felt so acutely by the sensitive, however obscure their origins or idealistic their aspirations may be.

Education

Institutional education at several levels, especially that of the ancient English universities of Oxford and Cambridge (and, by implication, others) is sharply and adversely criticized in *Jude*. Although elementary education had been made free by 1870 and by 1880 attendance was compulsory, the mass of working-class children was denied access to the educational ladder. Such access came through the endowed grammar schools dotted over the country; and especially from the fee-paying independent public schools. Hardy's own schooling ended at the age of sixteen, but the usual school-leaving age was fourteen – and at the rest of the poorer elementary schools, often lower. Most children were too useful as wage-earners to be allowed to enjoy long years of 'idleness': they were at best allowed to leave school to take up a long apprenticeship, during which they could earn some money to help out with the family budget.

Hardy himself (though his headmaster was an excellent teacher of Latin) was largely self taught: in this, as in many other ways, there is a great deal of Hardy in Jude. Characteristically, Hardy denied this: '. . . there is not a scrap of personal detail in it ... no book ... contained less' of his own life. Possibly very few of the events – but certainly many of his thoughts and feelings – are here evident.

At the opening of the novel, when Phillotson is about to leave (p.29), it is made clear that Jude, a bookish lad, is not a regular day-boy. He is far too useful (drawing water for Drusilla's bakery; and working – until sacked for feeding grain to the birds he is employed to scare away – in Farmer Troutham's fields) to enjoy the luxury of daytime school attendance. Note that the other scholars are much less endeared to the schoolmaster than one who knows him less and who, anyway, is fond of reading! Now we know from the indispensable Hardy biography by Florence Emily Hardy (first published in two volumes, and almost wholly prepared by Hardy himself) that he had made notes in 1888 for a short story about a young man 'who could not go to Oxford', who drove a cart, carried on his self-appointed studies, and asked Hardy to lend him his Latin Grammar: 'His struggles and ultimate failure. Suicide. There is something the world ought to be shown, and I am the one to show it to them – though I was not altogether hindered going, at least to Cambridge, and could have gone up easily at five-and-twenty.' This is clearly the germ of at least one facet of *Jude the Obscure*, and the basic notion of 'education' as a force that can lift someone out of his or her native background. Hardy had already illustrated this in previous novels, such as with Fancy Day in *Under The Greenwood Tree* (1872) and Eustacia Vye in *The Return of The Native* (1878). Of course, one is educated largely by experience: Jude learns an immediate lesson, very soon after the schoolmaster has told him to be kind to animals and birds, from the rough tongue and rougher hands of Farmer Troutham (p.35). But it is with the institutional aspect of learning and education, and not the 'University of Life' in general, that we are here principally concerned. This is bound up in our novel with Christminster, which is of course not just Oxford but essentially a vision, a 'city of youth and dreams'.

It is with the reality, however, and not the vision of this 'castle manned by scholarship and religion' (Part 1, Chapter 3) that the novel smoulders with the bitterness of frustration, class-consciousness, social and financial inequality, the power of an outworn system, the sense of depressed isolation. Jude, after all, with all his weaknesses, is a competent and avid scholar: note some areas of his reading (for example Part 1, Chapters 5 and 6), and his obvious familiarity with verse, prose and drama from antiquity to his own day. Yet by Chapter 2 of Part 2, daylight reveals the actual: 'something barbaric', 'wounded, broken', 'rottenness'; and he realizes that the stone-mason's yard 'was a centre of effort as worthy as that dignified by the name of scholarly study within the noblest of the colleges'. Paradoxically and ironically, his workaday labours help to maintain and reinforce the very strongholds that exclude him. He is separated from his happy and more fortunate young contemporaries by 'only a wall – but what a wall! . . . he was as far from them as if he had been at the antipodes'.

Jude soon discovers, rather belatedly it would seem, that one needs a qualifying entry, or must study and save for fifteen years, to enter these 'delusive precincts', and miserably recognizes his social and perhaps intellectual ineligibility. His destiny lies (so brusquely but sensibly emphasized by the only one of the five Masters who condescend to notice and reply to his enquiry) with 'the manual toilers ... the book of humanity' of the town, not the gown, life – the living, loving turmoil of ordinary citizens.

Hardy's development of this theme is then tinged with cynicism: as Jude indulges in his drinking-bout, the two devil-may-care young men with him are undergraduates, interested mainly in bull-pups, smoking, goading Jude on, not having the 'slightest conception of a single word' of his Latin. Sue, of course, considers Christminster non-intellectual and, in the modern jargon, 'élitist': 'The medievalism of Christminster must go, be sloughed off, or Christminster itself will have to go.' Jude has been 'elbowed off the pavement by the millionaires' sons'. By this time Jude has abandoned his academic and scholastic ambitions: but he continues his programme of self-education. Hitherto, before his 'burning of the books' (Part 4, Chapter 3) he had learned the harmonium (Phillotson never mastered his piano). In Part 5, Chapter 2 we read of Jude's attending a lecture on ancient history at a local public hall; and in Part 5, Chapter 6 he 'had a pretty zeal in the cause of education' by joining an Artizan's Mutual Improvement Society. Again a note of mockery creeps in. The group are of all creeds and denominations, 'their one common wish to enlarge their minds forming a sufficiently close bond of union'. But their narrow-minded bigotry forces Jude's immediate resignation.

It is in the last Part of the novel that Hardy summarizes much of his (and Jude's) sentiments. It is again Remembrance Day in all its splendour, and Jude is excited among the 'straw-hatted young men' and their well-dressed sisters up for the ceremony. Note the sporadic comments, such as 'meekly ignorant parents who had known no college in their youth', 'It do seem like the Judgement Day!', 'They are only learned Doctors'; and then it rains, and Jude, the 'Tutor of St Slums' holds forth, and his speech should be read closely. At the end of his analysis, what should happen to point a moral but that a belated Doctor, robed and panting, should have his cab-horse violently kicked in the belly. The rain falls on the poor family as they struggle to find lodgings: the atmosphere of the 'City of Light' darkens into ominous gloom: the outer stone walls of Sarcophagus College loom, throwing shadows of 'their four centuries of gloom, bigotry, and decay'. And it is here that the pitiable tragedy of the children's deaths occurs. The college organist is practising the 73rd Psalm (it is in parts movingly apt, and should be referred to briefly); two clergymen discuss the academic question of the altar, while 'all creation' is in lament.

The rest of Jude's existence is sombre and haunting: he sees again the phantoms of the past. He has heard that working-class students are to be helped into the University by 'schemes afoot for making the University less exclusive ... And it is too late, too late for me! Ah, and for how many worthier ones before me!' And for his son, too, Little Father Time, for whom he once had such excited hopes (Part 5, Chapter 3). Amid the happy summer preparation for the Remembrance Day, with the organ rehearsing, the concert beginning, the cheering at the games – all the gay whirl of the University fête, Jude dies with the sombre words of Job upon his parched lips.

The epigraph on the title page is 'The letter killeth'—the quotation (from Corinthians 3, 6) continues—'but the spirit giveth life.' In his treatment of what education in the formal sense can and ought to do, compared with what in fact it does attempt and achieve (as with other themes of the novel) Hardy tries to express the gulf between the vision and the dream, the ideal and the actual, the letter – formal, rigid and exclusive – and the spirit, the wider framework of opportunity and recognition of human aspirations: it is all part of Hardy's 'series of seemings' (Preface to First Edition). He exposes the reality behind and beneath the façade: the irony of Jude, the obscure mason, the equal and possibly superior in intellect and perseverance to many of the students, and perhaps some of their teachers. We are shown Jude: creative, purposeful, struggling to enter – even while restoring the very fabric of – a sterile, hostile, dead, élitist exclusiveness, alive only in its spectres of a once-glorious past. But 'the centre of thought and religion ... the intellectual and spiritual granary of this country', 'those palaces of light and learning' do not open their gates to such as he. His reality is an illusion.

In the 1912 Preface to *Jude*, Hardy wrote, 'I was informed that some readers thought ... that when Ruskin College (an Oxford College specifically for working-class students) was subsequently founded it should have been called the College of Jude the Obscure.' That must have given him great pleasure.

Finally, this theme strongly emphasizes Hardy's political view – and he was very much a radical – that a person should be judged by his actual and potential intrinsic worth, not by his class, speech, background, status or connections. Hardy himself never forgot his own 'peasant' origins and his determined struggles for recognition. Jude has many defects, but much of the impact and modern urgency of the novel derives from his hopeless battles against the inherent and bigoted conventions of a society that has been taught the wrong lessons.

Religion and nature

Hardy's personal attitude to the Church and religious practice permeates *Jude the Obscure*. He was in his own way, on a moral basis, a deeply religious man steeped in the Bible, a lover of hymn-singing and church music; but he could not accept institutionalized religion. It is possible that he was himself refused admission to the Church because of his lowly background and status (which would give an edge to some of his bitterness in the novel); in any case, he could not accept intellectually the notion of a good and lovable God, nor such principles as the Churches' condemnation of the unbaptized or bastard child ('The letter killeth...'): the Established Church he found élitist, status-oriented, distant from the mass of ordinary people whom it is supposed to serve – it lacked proper humility. In *Jude*, of course, there is particular focus on the marriage laws (See Notes, first Theme, *Marriage*).

Hardy rejected Christian theology. The notions of God or Providence, or life after death, were to him intellectually untenable. Some of this was clearly derived from early personal experiences of the obvious cruelty of man's and Nature's laws (hanging, animal suffering), some from contemporary scientific and political thought (Spencer, Huxley, J. S. Mill, Darwin, Hume), some from philosophers such as Schopenhauer and Hartmann; but much more from *The Saturday Review* (founded 1855), which was for long his favourite journal. Some of the articles were written by one of his great friends and advisers, Horace Moule, a brilliant scholar and reviewer with whom Hardy often discussed modern thought. Not capable of passing in Mathematics, he left both Oxford and Cambridge without a degree, and his failure drove him to drink and eventual suicide: a death which shattered Hardy. There may well be something of Moule in Jude; Hardy's sombre cast of mind may, in part, have derived from the connection. It is a certainty, however, that the brilliantly-written *Review* exposed many forms of hypocrisy and smug sentimentality; derided the notion of standards of morality and dealt with social evils of all kinds. It ridiculed the sentimental middle-class view of morality and village life, and all forms of religious excess; it was sceptical, deflating, pricking the bubble of Victorian pomposity; it was rationalistic and thought-provoking. It suited, and doubtless influenced, Hardy's attitudes.

Thus Hardy's 'philosophy' excluded God: the universe was neutral or indifferent but could be malignant. He believed (as did every good Victorian) that 'the wages of sin is death'; but, less conventionally, that mankind was prone to disappointment and pain, strife and melancholy, in the huge, impersonal mechanism of a relentless Nature. One's fate was largely pre-determined: no one can escape his deserts and destiny. Thus are Hardy's characters subject to what they may believe to be chance and coincidence, just as Hardy himself believed. But there are vast forces ranged against his characters, from which there is no evasion or escape: they are shown as puppets manipulated by a grand scheme beyond their will.

> As flies to wanton boys are we to the gods;
> They kill us for their sport.

Gloucester's terrible comment in Shakespeare's *King Lear* seems to underlie much of the 'Hardeian philosophy' of life, except that he would probably have substituted 'fates' for 'gods'. There is no struggling clear from one's past: one must reap the whirlwind; much of that rings true in our novel in that the principal characters suffer, in Jude's words, and the use of the Biblical phrasing deepens the irony (p.327): '. . . a cloud that has gathered over us . . . wronged no man, corrupted no man, defrauded no man . . . done that which was right in our own eyes'. From that moment, their sufficient wretchedness descends swiftly into tragedy.

Now this may not be an accurate, or even a powerful, analysis of human life – but it was Hardy's, as it was that of the ancient Greeks that Hardy loved so well, and about whom he knew and read so much. And it does, of course, affect his characterization. Coupled with this runs a cynical, sceptical (though not callous) view of human happiness, especially where this is conventionally linked with religion, love and marriage. The blind 'Immanent Will' renders much of human activity and striving negative, ironic, and regrettably painful. As Hardy wrote, 'Pain has been and pain is. No new sort of morals in Nature can remove pain from the past or make it pleasure to those who bore it. So either . . . Nature is blind, or an automaton, and you only throw responsibility a stage farther back'; and, 'I have been looking for God 50 years, and I think that if he had existed I should have discovered him.' So it is not remarkable that in *Jude* we have full measure of a pessimism that excluded a God of Love; the universe is indifferent and hostile: it is all a struggle for recognition and survival over hurdles of cruelty, disease and suffering. Only human 'charity', genuine loving kindness, can save mankind from its own toils, can help at least – but not through outworn superstition or ritual.

Throughout the novel, as Jude's and Sue's attachment to and severance from conventional religion swings its fateful changes, references, often ironically conveyed, abound to the staleness and outworn distance of the creeds of conventional religion. Note the last sentence on p.31; the carter's view of Christminster as a seed-bed of parsons (p.44); some of his books come from an 'insolvent clergyman of the neighbourhood' (p.54), and just as Jude is inflating himself with the depth and breadth of his academic book-list, with a quotation from Matthew springing readily from his lips, the pig's pizzle slaps his ear (p.58).

Such references abound, but it is, of course, with the entry of Sue Bridehead into the story, with her modern and arch

views, that the anti-clerical emphasis becomes more notice-
able. She is first seen (Part 2, Chapter 2) in a highly conventional Anglican setting among religious books and objects,
prompting Jude to admire her 'sweetly, saintly Christian
business'; then (in the next chapter) we find her at worship
in the Cathedral church of Christminster of Cardinal College
itself. But she buys the pagan images, displays them promi-
nently and reads her very non-conformist Gibbon, thus defying
all convention. Sue's views on the model of Jerusalem are
pointed (Part 2, Chapter 5), as is Jude's recital of the Creed
in the tavern (Chapter 7), though the event propels him
towards the ministry rather than the academic City of Light
– a twist of the irony here. Sue's views on the Cathedral
(Part 3, Chapter 1), Jude's seeing her almost as a divinity
(end of Chapter 3) lead into her explicit condemnation of
all that Christminster is supposed to stand for (Chapter 4)
– all her conversation and responses here are significant.
During the sequence of her marriage to Phillotson this incompatibility of 'the letter and the spirit' of the marriage bond
remains poised, in balance, as yet not worked through;
in that interim Jude's experiences with the speculative, com-
mercially-minded hymn-writer (Chapter 10) are wryly ironic.

It is at Shaston – note the epigraph on the part-title page
(219) – that so much of significance occurs relative to this
theme (and, indeed, most of the other essential elements of
the tragedy). Note the last line of Part 4, Chapter 1, the first
of Chapter 2, Jude's destruction of his theological and ethical
works in Chapter 3; and again, the plot turns more on the
marriage laws so resisted by Sue than on the broader aspects
of religious dissension. The churchwarden's story (Part 5,
Chapter 6) underlies the superstitious turn of mind of the
ostensibly devout, and Jude's and Sue's moral ostracism: 'O
why should Nature's law be mutual butchery!' (p.327). Note
that Arabella, of all people, now espouses chapel-worship
(Chapters 7 and 8).

The death by hanging and suicide of the three children, and the still birth, give the final bitter twist of Fate in a hostile world – the trapped victims cannot escape alive. Against a background of church music and academic irrelevance the full horror emerges the more stark and harrowing ... 'Fate has given us this stab in the back for being such fools as to take Nature at her word!' (Part 6, Chapter 2, p.358), and Sue recants in penance. The encounter in the church, in Chapter 3, is highly charged, and reaches its natural conclusion in Jude's lingering death and Sue's physical and moral sacrifice in her renewed (but now physical) relationship with Phillotson. Bitter circumstances and the 'letter' of the law have finally killed her remarkable spirit.

One of the early critics of *Jude* (and one of Hardy's great friends) was Edmund Gosse, who wrote in the journal *Cosmopolis*, (January 1896), 'What has Providence done to Mr. Hardy that he should rise up in the arable land of Wessex and shake his fist at his creator?' But the sensitive and kindly Gosse, who found the novel otherwise irresistible, clearly did not share Hardy's disturbing and uncompromising view of institutional religion. Are we convinced that such a situation is *possible*? Can hostile intentions surround one's life, so that we hear the outcry of a child, 'I ought not to be born, ought I?' (Part 6, Chapter 1, p.351); and of a mother, 'It is no use fighting against God' (p.362), and 'My children—are dead ... They were sin-begotten ... their death was the first stage of my purification' (p.383). If such things can be said, if such situations are possible, if humans can be so trapped, then perhaps one can at least sympathize – though not necessarily identify oneself wholly – with Hardy's intellectual agnosticism. It is, after all, as he said in his Preface to the First Edition (p.23 in the present edition), 'a deadly war waged between flesh and spirit'.

It may finally be suggested that, in a novel studded with biblical references, what seems a deliberate pattern emerges towards the end in which Jude's fate parallels that of Christ: all the later references are to the New Testament. There is great stress on Corinthians, Hardy's favourite Book of the Bible, of which he said, 'Its verses will stand fast when all the rest that you call religion has passed away'. There is emphasis on the lack of human and communal charity, a sense of trial and exposure to hostility – creation groaning and darkening near the last hours; and Jude, like Christ, asks for water and dies untended. But there is little sense of hope to come. Jude and Sue first met near the Martyrs' Cross: in Part 4, Chapter 5 Jude protests, 'Crucify me, if you will!' and other specific references to the Cross and Jerusalem abound. Sue 'will drink her cup to the dregs', and Jude wishes, like Job, that he had never been born. But neither achieves peace: Jude dies physically; Sue spiritually; and no sense of resurrection prevails.

Sexuality

Sexuality as it applies to the major characters will be considered under that Section, but a brief comment in general may be useful. Many of the plots (and therefore the characters) of Hardy's novels are dominated by the passions of men and women in love: in short, by sexual longing and possession. Once the word 'sex' has been shorn of all its commercialized, sensational, ugly or otherwise debased associations, it can be seen that it is with justice that Hardy has been called 'the father of the sex novel'. We find some of the torment and agony caused by and for love; how some are sacrificed and humiliated because of it, and others purified and elevated; how there is a true love and a false love, the difference never easily nor readily recognized; how love can ennoble, degrade; kindle worthy or ignoble passions. In the major Wessex novels, this factor often helps to make the plots and characters akin to those in many of the old ballads of English literature, so dearly loved and so sharply remembered by Hardy from his boyhood and youth.

Here, however, *Jude* – in this as in so many other ways – is an exception. Here the tone is sharper; the focus narrower and more intense; the depth more psychological; the attitude more modern and the facts less veiled. Hardy, in presenting this conflict between 'flesh and spirit', did not hesitate to dwell on the flesh so as to shock Victorian prudishness and hypocrisy on the one side, enabling him to elevate and contrast the other: 'I feel that the animal side of human nature should never be dwelt on except as a contrast or foil to its spiritual side'. Much of the novel hinges on the essential problem of intimate sexual relationship and its consequences, and Hardy wished to expose and exploit the real, not the artificial or romanticized; revealing, so far as he was able, what he considered to be the wickedness of English sexual conventions. In this he was uncompromising.

As early as Part 1, Chapter 2, in describing the scene of the newly-seeded corn-field, Hardy details its earthy associations, quite divorced from any romantic historic past. 'Love-matches that had populated the adjoining hamlets had been made up there between reaping and carrying. Under the hedge which divided the field ... girls had given themselves to lovers who would not turn their heads to look at them by the next harvest...'. The carter in the next chapter mentions, along with the scholars and parsons of Christ-minster, the 'wenches in streets o' nights'; Vilbert has his 'female pills' (Chapter 4); and with the introduction of Arabella Donn in Chapter 6 the references to overt sexuality accumulate and begin to give this aspect of the novel its particular force, character and direction.

Outside and beyond the (separately-considered) major characters and themes, note the following relevant references: the 'scores of coupled earth-worms' (Part 1, Chapter 2); the picture of Samson and Delilah in the Alfredston inn (Chapter

7) and its obvious appropriateness; in the same chapter, the comment of a man about lovers and homeless dogs out in all weathers; the talk of Arabella's friends and the attitude of the gossip and Arabella's parents at the beginning of Chapter 8.

Note also the clientele of the Christminster public house at the end of Chapter 6 in Part 2; the attitude of the girls and staff of the Training-school (Part 3, Chapter 3); and the scene at the Registry Office (Part 5, Chapter 4). Of course, the theme by now is so intertwined with the marriage topic (see first Theme, *Marriage*) and the characters themselves that its emphasis is abundantly clear and obviously crucial to the development of the remaining story.

Within the bounds of this novel – with enough material unexploited for several subsequent works, never to be written in prose – Hardy had explored this theme considerably. By no means a profound thinker, and inevitably unaware of the Freudian impact on the study of sexuality (not to emerge until the turn of the century) he had elaborated it as far as he could – and at times, it must be said, a little falteringly and creakingly. But it is significant that D. H. Lawrence in his *Study of Thomas Hardy* grasped the strength of his attack on the established conventions of 'bourgeois morality'. It is an inevitable conclusion that after *Jude the Obscure* this fundamental human theme was vigorously and richly extended in Lawrence's *Sons and Lovers* and *The Rainbow* and developed in his later novels; the hostility they provoked forced Lawrence into near-lifelong exile from his native England. Hardy considered *Jude* 'a moral book', but he also knew that 'Britons hate ideas'. *Jude*, among other distinctive credits, must be reckoned as the boldest of his experiments.

Structure

In common with all but the most eccentric creative artists
– whether in words, music or other media – a novelist must
envisage a structure, a shape, to fulfil his intentions and eventual purpose. He must create a sense of place, time, motive,
into which his characters fit credibly: and he must, within
this framework, present his ideas and bring the whole to a
meaningful end. He must thus have a formula (or even a set
of formulae) to accomplish this. A few points about Hardy's
structure in *Jude* may be useful, though they cannot be
exhaustive. This would demand an independent analysis of
every theme in its inter-relationship with every character in
great detail, so as fully to expose the often incredibly intricate
patterns of complex linking. The skill of a great novelist consists
to a large extent in managing this smoothly, so that gaps and
'creaking' in the plot are not obvious.

Broadly speaking, there is an architectural quality about
the structure of *Jude* (in itself not surprising, considering
Hardy's profession, that of his father and of Jude himself).
Hardy's intention was a novel of 'all contrasts': 'Sue and her
heathen gods set against Jude's reading the Greek Testament;
Christminster academical, Christminster in the slums; Jude
the saint, Jude the sinner; Sue the Pagan, Sue the saint;
marriage, no marriage; etc., etc.' Nothing could be more
explicit. In this way there is a 'geometry' of opposing tensions
among the four major characters, bringing out the conflict
in this 'deadly war waged between flesh and spirit'. There
is a shifting of depth and emphasis; there are moments of
attraction and repulsion, of granting then withdrawing sympathy, of description against dialogue, of movement against
rest, and so on. The basic criss-crossing of this aspect of the
structure is best illustrated by concrete examples.

Look at the end of Chapter 3 in Part 2. Sue is reading her anti-clerical Gibbon, having set up her pagan statuettes against a Calvary crucifixion print. She settles down to sleep, but cannot rest, and wakes at intervals, sometimes when the clock is striking, to see the idols against the cross. Simultaneously, Jude is staying up for extra study of his Greek New Testament, hearing the same bell tolling, speaking aloud the incantation of a sacred prayer of intense belief. Think of what Jude knows of Sue: she knows nothing of him. Think of what we know about both of them. Similarly, for a further example when their relationships have developed, take the scene of the children's visit to the religious exhibition at Christminster in Chapter 5, and how the characters view the model of Jerusalem in the presence of the innocence and inexperience of the schoolchildren.

The adults have each a different perspective: Jude is absorbed and uncritical; Sue is detached and highly critical, yet she remembers the model, later on, in detail. Both men react to her originality. Again, one must think of what is known by each about the other: *not* what Hardy has told us, the readers, but what they have themselves experienced of each other's company and conversation. And remember what we know of their backgrounds – their hopes and fears, and so on. In this way the building up of tensions, the parallelling of experience, gives us depth of characterization within a structure, itself part of the whole design of the plot and purpose.

Of course, the major themes are intertwined with the characters: in a way, in this concentrated novel, the themes are the characters, and vice-versa; they cannot be separated off. It would be an interesting exercise (and is recommended, once the novel has been well absorbed) to chart diagrammatically the pattern of theme against character. Tabulate the major themes as headings (religion, education, marriage, and so on), list the characters in a column, and see how each links vertically and horizontally: by reference, actual experience, involvement, positive or negative action or reaction. Decide whether the theme is accepted conventionally or not, is a background or dominant feature. This would reveal not merely the holding and structuring of a complex pattern with considerable success, but the overall density and compactness of the entire work.

A deliberate reference to structure is of course given by Hardy's place-names, which indicate the parts and sequences of the entire pattern of the novel. It establishes the idea of movement and general rootlessness, and helps grip together what otherwise might have been a sprawl of events, and motives This device is so integral to Hardy's structure that it does not need detailed analysis: but it is to be noted how Part 4, *At Shaston*, is a watershed – it is a crucial area where threads are gathered up and a new direction given: it wipes the slate clean, so to speak, but prepares for the eventual 'catastrophe', in the dramatic sense, of the whole story.

It will be further commented upon (in the Section on *Style*) that with so much interweaving, and so many themes in action together, the structure bends and creaks a little, as if unable to hold the weight or maintain its grasp on all its material. There is a great deal of short-circuiting by chance and coincidence, though these do indeed happen in real life. But there is a very heavy – at times contrived-seeming – dependence on endless journeys and correspondence, and Arabella's 'popping up' at crucial moments to give the plot a decisive wrench. And Little Father Time, a fascinating creature, seems to exist solely to kill off the unnamed children, and so to set the scene for the final tragedy. But a scaffolding is there: there is a structure, a geometry – or, to use another term from the physical sciences, a balance and tension of forces. The pivot or lever used to apply the stress will vary from place to place, from event to event, and from one character to another – but an overall sense of pattern and design inevitably emerges to hold a mass of material together. It is not entirely integrated: it is perhaps overloaded. And, whether by the author's conscious purpose or not, the book's own structural shortcomings help to reinforce the picture of the fractured society it has set out to analyse.

Style

'Style' is a simple single word: but it covers an enormous range, and is a key-point of the writer's craft. The ways in which an author can express his thoughts and create his world are diverse and often complex. Our text is that of a long novel, crammed with ideas and intention, with many-sided characters: it comes as the last of a long series of novels, and its particular purpose and flavour is unique and distinctive. It would be foolish, therefore, to attempt any simple analysis of Hardy's style, or to base a general estimate on any one single aspect or part of the whole work. Sooner or later, one must get down to fundamental elements, even down to words and phrasing, before one can assume a unified view of the total style.

It may be best to consider first some of the obvious weaknesses. To begin with, this style is allusive. A glance at the textual Notes will confirm this at once. Solely on the literary aspect there are nearly fifty allusions to, quotations from, or phrasing demanding a knowledge of, the Old and New Testaments: seven from classical authors, and at least thirty from English and European writers over the centuries. There are names and terms from the world of painting and architecture, philosophy ethics and Biblical criticism, and quotations in Greek and Latin. Now it is of course true that the educated novel-reading public of the time would not be unduly put out by this: but some examples of such allusions are extreme even for the well-educated, such as: (Postscript, 1912 – see p.25) 'Diderot's words', 'Bludyer'; some dialect not explicit from the context; and such veiled allusions as in Part 2 Chapter 1 to the Christminster spectres, and so on. All these have been made part and parcel of the running prose, and send one scuttling to reference-books (not necessarily a bad

thing, of course) to elucidate the author's meaning. Some of
this seems rather like a display of knowledge for its own sake
(often found in the unsure self-educated writer striving to
prove his intellectual background and status); and it must
be said that in *Jude* Hardy is, in fact, much less allusive than
in some of the earlier Wessex novels. But do characters,
however much educated and by whatever process, actually
talk like Sue and Jude? Most of the dialogue, in fact, seems
stilted: the characters are lecturing one another; even Phillotson, talking to his friend Gillingham (p.252), manages, in the
course of only two sentences, to introduce the names of four
characters from literature.

Similarly, there is often verbosity and redundance; ponder-
ous words; clumsy polysyllabic and unhappy phrases – which
a little patience could have ironed out into smoother, simpler
writing. Again, there is much less of this in *Jude* than in many
of the previous novels; but a random sampling must include
such words as 'tassets', 'centrifugal', 'interstices', 'scintil-
lations', 'law of transmutation' and so on, all within the first
four chapters. There are clichés easily avoidable: Melchester
Cathedral was 'the most graceful architectural pile in England'; and some ungainly split infinitives: 'to hastily tidy',
'to honestly and legally marry'. Some patches are extra-
ordinarily tortuous: 'conjunctive orders', 'midnight conti-
guity', 'through the varieties of spirituous delectation', Sue
'blinked away an access of eye moisture', 'the antagonisms
of sex to sex were left without any counterpointing predilec-
tions'. Some of this seems to indicate a flagging of patience
or imagination, perhaps a little academic pretentiousness, an
over-forcing of himself or his characters to elevate the speech
or writing into what might be considered acceptable rather
than what is natural.

We have already noted that, in places, the mechanism of
the novel is clumsy: the plot tends to creak with occasional
stretches of coincidence, especially around Arabella. There

are touches of melodrama, too, with constant climaxes, but a great deal of this was consequent upon the book's original serial construction.

Not to mention this debit side is to be uncritical; but to over-emphasize it would be even more unsound. For Hardy never pretended to be a master of language (or of anything, indeed, in his natural quiet modesty). The virtues of his style far outweigh these flaws, which have, of course, been carefully and deliberately extracted. These may well present, as Blunden wrote, 'remarkable spasms of contorted and straggling English' and reveal 'inartistic knottiness', but over its entire range, Hardy's is a strikingly direct and forceful style, of great pressure and versatility. He had his own characteristic view: 'The whole secret of a living style and the difference between it and a dead style, lies in not having too much style – being, in fact, a little careless, or rather seeming to be, here and there. It brings wonderful life into the writing.' But there are other factors to be considered. After the hostile reception of his *Tess of the D'Urbervilles* (1891); Hardy commented, 'If this sort of thing continues, no more novel-writing for me.' And the serial of *Jude* had to undergo heavy censoring and 'softening'; then the one-volume edition involved Hardy in wearisome re-editing and revision: he had even written to the publishers asking for the contract to be cancelled. And, as we have noted, the published work provoked a storm of hostile comment. He admitted to having lost the 'energy for revising and improving': that in writing *Jude* his mind 'was fixed on the ending', which might explain some of the 'stretching' of coincidence and sporadic loss of imaginative steering; and some loss of grip in maintaining the overall interest. He felt, perhaps, that he done enough through the novel, or taken it as far as he could: that it would be in poetry (his first and possibly strongest love) that he could express himself the more deeply and powerfully. *Jude* is in fact particularly memorable for its small patches of intense pictorial symbolic 'snapshots' –

of people and places and crucial moments, e.g. the boy in the fields; the distant view of Christminster; the encounter with Arabella; the rabbit in the trap; Little Father Time and the death-scene. This 'series of seemings' appears as a natural bridge towards the more metaphorical and intense concentration into narrative and lyrical verse.

There is, in fact, strong evidence that the harsh prose of *Jude*, only occasionally clumsy, is deliberate. Hardy believed in the necessity of disproportion: 'Art is a disproportioning (i.e. distorting, throwing out of proportion) of realities, to show more clearly the features that matter in those realities, which, if merely copied or reported inventorially, might possibly be observed, but would more probably be overlooked.' This view applies to all Hardy's work, but especially to *Jude*; it is a key to all his thought: 'This reproduction is achieved by seeing into the *heart of a thing*.' Much of the style of *Jude* is harsh, doggedly akward, without charm: it suited the special nature of the story. It is a breakaway from tradition and convention in style as well as in overall intention. Wishing to exploit the 'deadly war' of flesh and spirit with all his art, Hardy seemed deliberately to deny himself any aesthetic pleasure in his imaginative creation. He wanted *Jude* to disturb, to grate, to jolt and shock; and to achieve this he used every device he had developed. Perhaps, too, in so doing he realized that he could go no further in this medium: one can distort for the truth only so far. And the antagonism aroused clinched the issue.

All this must not, however, detract from the considerable qualities of Hardy's style: indeed, it underlines it. There is power and impact here: it can convey deep emotions; the dry, almost abstract, prose wields considerable force. This is best studied through concrete examples.

Look at Part 1, Chapter 2, p.33, beginning at, 'The brown surface of the field . . .' and ending, p.34, with '. . . they much resembled his own.' Remembering what has led up to this

moment, note the visual clarity of the scene, and how Hardy
has conveyed its dullness, its uniformity, its atmosphere of
depression – ending with a morbid touch about the lad's 'dead
family'. He expresses his own sense of frustration, of not meaning anything, of not being anybody: 'How ugly it is here!'
Note the long paragraph that follows, and how it suggests a
'meanly utilitarian', unprogressive, unhistoric area: look at
the negative words throughout, such as: depriving, bickering,
weariness; and the account of the reality, if not the crudity,
of unmeaning love. Isolation is stressed, of the place, the
orphan child, of life in a vacuum: his only friends the birds,
to whom he must deny subsistence – his aunt shows less interest
in him than they; and when he lets them feed he feels at one
with them and enjoys the sense of belonging to something
– like his, their lives are 'puny and sorry'.

In this simple and obvious example we have great visual
and emotional clarity: an exactly precise setting of external
nature; and of an inner consciousness neatly, deftly, quickly
portrayed. And by this stylistic device various themes of life
and character have already subtly been promoted for later
development.

Another example: take the opening description of Shaston
in Part 4, Chapter 1. This Part of the book is to be crucial
in its treatment of theme and character: it is a major staging-
post in the general drifting and rootlessness of the story. The
description up to the point of Jude's entering the scene is
a set-piece of Hardy's 'new' style and approach: there is no
comforting atmosphere here, as would be expected in the
earlier Wessex novels. The prose, like the place, is dry: the
tone is precise and wry. What glory there was has been 'ruth-
lessly swept away'; the aura is one of melancholy, of a great
past not merely dead and buried, but forgotten – it is a place
'virtually unvisited'. There are strong negatives: 'impossible',
'hardly accessible', 'world-forgotten'; and then a sense of
corruption – the hawkers trading in water, the toiling animals,

with 'more wanton women than honest wives and maids' –
and the arch comment about the necessity of irreligion,
'bemoaned' over cups of beer, considered by Hardy as an
example of their sense of humour; and finally the rootlessness
of the wandering fairground and market traders and followers,
wintering there as if in bird-like migration. And it was to this
'breezy and whimsical spot' that Jude made his way. The
presentation is all of a piece in its intention: comfortless, with
deliberate underplaying of the sense of isolation and loss –
precisely what Jude will experience during his stay there.

Finally, as an example of Hardy's flexibility of stylistic skill,
the arrival of Little Father Time is remarkable. Although he
will later be studied as a separate character, it is worth looking
for a moment at his presentation in the second half of Chapter 3
in Part 5. Note the physical description of his size and pallor:
his physical childishness combined with a mental precocity
– his loneliness and lifelessness; and look especially (p.295)
at the paragraph beginning 'He was Age...' It is poetic,
abstract, symbolic. He, too, is another wanderer, quickly sent
off again by his mother (the ticket-collector feels 'the unfitness
of things'); and he walks off into the night, mechanically but
impersonally. The whole scene sets the macabre, other-
worldly, near-grotesque atmosphere that is to surround his
living, and horribly his dead, presence in the remainder of
the story.

Characters

There are no spare characters in Jude – such as those, for example, littering the pages of Dickens or Scott. The characters interpret the themes – are the personalization of the themes – in depth and throughout the story. The original serial form of publication doubtless dictated certain patterns of characterization, such as the gradual introduction of the characters, until their personalities and inter-relationships are firmly established before each one plays out his full role. Note how, in the first chapter of Part 1, we are shortly and sharply introduced to Mr Phillotson and the Christminster theme; then some villagers; the lad Jude, placed in his 'ugly' setting; and the old woman Drusilla Fawley. In Chapter 2, other detail is quickly provided – hints of Jude's family background; Sue is mentioned; the unfeeling atmosphere is stressed through Farmer Troutham; and so on. Patterns are laid down and begin to unfold.

It must next be noted that, in order to sense the full nature of the characters, a firm understanding is needed of Hardy's basic themes: these have already been detailed; their inter-twining sets the mould in which the characters are formed. Here, too, the Notes on *Structure* should be consulted, especially with regard to the balancing and counterpoise Hardy has arranged. After all, the novelist must select his 'slice of life' and try to depict the participants credibly; so some shaping of his material is vital. In Hardy's words, this novel was an endeavour 'to give shape and coherence to a series of seemings' (See Hardy's Preface, p.23) and, under the immense stresses borne by the principal characters, a sense of firm structure must bind them, and the 'plot' they play out, maintaining a pattern of reasonable, recognizable reality.

The formula adopted here is as follows. First there will be

a brief note on the possible 'prototypes' of the character to be analysed. All Hardy's work bears the stamp of his personal history: the men and women he creates stem from his own life and background: his relationships; family and friends; village gossip and tradition; his accumulated knowledge of local history and dialect. All these interpenetrate his portraits, and give them an added, sharper point: of course, not every character can or need be so identified. Then, again wherever possible and available, Hardy's own views on a particular character will be briefly mentioned. Finally, a developed character-sketch will be presented.

A word of caution. No interpretation of character in a novel can be final or utterly objective: *Jude* is a particularly controversial novel; and the critical reader must, as much as possible, bring his own feelings and opinions to bear on the novel (and on these Notes).

Jude Fawley
'I am a chaos of principles'

There are some obvious similarities between Jude and his creator: a boyhood unwillingness to grow up, an early lack of ambition and hesitancy over choosing a means of livelihood, and then an overwhelming desire for self-improvement through what may be called an 'academic' régime of classical and literary study. There is, too, a great eagerness for life, a thirst for happiness (a theme which runs through many of Hardy's novels), a brooding curiosity over heredity and its possibly hampering effects, and eventually a realization of the human struggle for survival in an apparently hostile universe.

However, Hardy's approach to Jude's character and story was undoubtedly affected by other factors. The Biblical Book of *Jude* discusses victims of sin; the Fawley surname is taken from the village of that name, the home of many of his ancestors. Hardy's first name for Jude, in the draft of the novel, was Jack Head, a distant relation, a parish-boy who was, in fact, a bird-scarer. In part, too, Jude reflects the husband of his aunt Mary (herself remembered in Marygreen), an interesting, rather wild character, a self-taught cobbler who dreamt of going to college; he, too, had a 'mass of black, curly hair' (p.96), and had learnt enough Latin to open a 'Latin school' locally. Like that of Jude, his death was hastened by a weakness for drink; he died, in fact, after spending a night in a ditch after a drunken bout – all this is reminiscent of Jude's violent alternations of mood and tendencies, and his eventual fate.

Again, the life and death of Hardy's brilliant scholar-friend, Horace Moule (see Notes p.23) certainly coloured his description of Jude's intellectual aspirations. He, too, despite his learning, lived a life strongly punctuated by excessive drink and sexual indulgence: his suicide undoubtedly sharpened the brooding, introspective and morbid element of our character and the book in general.

Jude, like Sue, in this 'series of seemings' lives out a paradox and an illusion. He personifies the struggle between passion and intellect, the flesh and the spirit: despite enormous problems and difficulties he masters languages and literature utterly above and beyond what could be expected of a man of his heredity and upbringing; yet he longs for and fondly cherishes an illusion, a vision – first of Christminster, then of a lesser vocation, despite the obvious social and financial barriers, which will ensure that he must and will remain obscure. He fails to see, until it is too late, the obvious façade and charade of much, if not most, of the institutional education and religion of his day. Yet, alongside this pure idealistic love for a vision, quite unselfish and disinterested, runs an intense sexual, physical urge, which he cannot easily control and which, essentially, ruins his life. Nor is this helped by a too-easy escape into the forgetfulness of excessive drinking: at times both his sexuality and drunkenness appal him. But he remains susceptible to them almost to the end; and both combine to destroy him.

More broadly, Jude symbolizes the tragic theme of man and his predicament: Hardy called him a 'poor puppet' and, in a letter to his friend Gosse, suggested that Jude showed 'the contrast between the ideal life a man wished to lead and the squalid life he was forced to lead'. This is a tragedy of unfulfilled aims, especially of the uprooted working-class intellectual: Jude is, indeed, the first working-class hero of serious fiction. The very fact of his being isolated from his class makes him at once more solitary, more alienated. When he is sober, devoid of what he calls 'erotolepsy', he is sensitive and high-principled, and thus the more aware of his situation. This charges some scenes with intense poignancy, such as that of the rabbit in the gin (pp.234–6): for love and for his intellectual striving Jude is prepared to give up his all. But both are visionary ideals, both are unattainable in the particular situation which has developed. He and Sue alike are trapped, snared, and may be – perhaps must be – destroyed by hostile forces outside themselves.

It must be said, perhaps harshly, that his fixation, either on the scholastic or sexual ideal, disables him. Sometimes he seems lacking in intelligence, even common sense. He rarely takes the obvious or adequate measure to deal with a specific situation. How could someone read and study so much and yet learn so little of the world? What potential undergraduate would choose his College and course by observing 'an elderly gentleman ... walking in the public path of a parklike enclosure'? And then noting to whom he will address his letter of appeal (if not application) by looking at various senior scholars, 'and from those he ultimately selected five whose physiognomies seemed to say to him that they were appreciative and far-seeing men' (Part 2, Chapter 6, p.134)? He is blinded and narrowed by his piety (even though he has already been inflamed by lust for a woman) to an extraordinary degree: he sees Sue lettering texts, and this makes her work 'A sweet, saintly, Christian business': Sue becomes 'almost a divinity' (p.165). He is outraged by her application of scholarship towards the standard New Testament. Now such piety and bigotry seem absurd in one who so readily yields to the gratification of lesser, baser impulses. Sometimes he is negligently stupid, especially when the old Christminster dream stirs again (Part 6, Chapter 1, pp.342–51); when, after asserting that the family must first establish themselves in lodgings, he neglects to do so in a boyish, even childlike gesture – making speeches in the rain, delaying their settling down. This directly causes the split-up of the young family which leads to the death of the children.

Jude is, nevertheless, a compelling hero with many healthy qualities: he is tenacious and honest; he hurts no one. He is surely a romantic, an idealist beaten and trapped by circumstances. Practical reality means little to him. Perhaps he is foredoomed: certainly all the 'Establishment' forces are ranged against him; perhaps his ideals are unattainable and he constantly deceives himself. But he has principles. They may veer and change, but even the changes are made after great stress, without hypocrisy: he will always persist in what he deems to be right.

One shares Jude's few moments of joy, and dreads his naiveté and vulnerability in a harsh, changing, ever more materialistic environment. It could be that he is punished overmuch for his excesses – and for his innocent lack of adjustment to the powerful forces of traditional convention and agonizing social change: he is torn and shattered between these stresses. He is crushed by poverty: he is no match for Sue (and who is or could be?) either intellectually or as a lover–husband. But we must feel for him. We are outraged by the waste of a struggling human talent, and oppressed by the continual denial of happiness, accomplishment and security. It is an indictment of society and institutions that

Jude should taste life so bitterly, down to the dregs: it is poignant that he should even continue to hope, against all odds – and almost at his last breath – that the future may hold out more promise and light to others of his kind. That he should lose the will to live and wish, like Job, that he had never been born, is unendurably, tragically sombre and pitiful.

Susanna Bridehead

'. . . an urban miss is what you are'

Whereas the character of Jude Fawley is fundamentally straightforward, that of Sue Bridehead is complex, and her 'origins' are similarly diverse and interpenetrating. Her first name recalls The History of Susanna, a book of the Apocrypha, which tells how Susanna was accused of adultery by certain Jewish elders who had themselves unsuccessfully threatened her chastity: eventually her innocence was proved, and her accusers put to death. She, as Jude's cousin, is of the Fawley side of the family, and the village of that name (Great Fawley) was the birthplace of Hardy's grandmother Mary Head, who died when he was seventeen: the 'Mary' appears in the Marygreen of our story. Somehow, too, one imagines that the compound 'Bridehead' is significant: 'bride' is what Sue is most unwilling to become, and the whole name is perhaps an ironic twist of 'maidenhead' – her almost neurotic concern for her personal chastity is a paramount feature of her personality and outlook.

Then there is the important element of Hardy's cousin Tryphena Sparks, almost certainly referred to in the preface to the First Edition: 'some of the circumstances being suggested by the death of a woman in the former year' (1890). Like Jude and Sue, they were cousins, and Tryphena became a schoolteacher, later a headmistress; and Hardy in his youth fell in love with her. Whether they ever became formally engaged is not known: it has been seriously suggested that she bore Hardy an illegitimate child previous to her marriage to a Charles Gale (three years after Hardy's own marriage to Emma Gifford). Much of this is hypothetical: what is undoubtedly true and verifiable is that Tryphena – a clever and emancipated girl who had lifted herself out of the working class into a position with status and independence – enjoyed a special relationship with Hardy, which he long cherished. To read more into their association is merely to speculate on the unknowable. Hardy, secretive by nature, never revealed openly and unambiguously his deepest feelings: and he was always susceptible to women, especially to those of dignity and intelligence.

When he was fifty-three he met the Honourable Florence Ellen Hungerford Milnes Henniker, aged thirty-seven, who was married to an officer in the Coldstream Guards. She was of the nobility and gentry: Hardy derived from much 'baser' stock, and (perhaps for that reason) strongly enjoyed such elevated and flattering company. He found her 'a clever intuitive woman' and was for a time drawn into her literary and political circle, though he did not share her High-Church Protestant beliefs, which he openly derided. She had written some novels and stories, was compassionate, horrified at brutality; despite her social status she retained an ironical and sceptical view of accepted institutions and conventions. There can be little doubt that this elegant and intellectual lady enjoyed Hardy's company and engaged his attentions, rather more than did his own wife. Hardy drew something of her into Sue, his most intellectual heroine. In a letter to Mrs Henniker he admitted that, 'I am more interested in the Sue story than in any I have written.' He insisted elsewhere that 'there is nothing perverted or depraved in Sue's nature ... (she) is a type of woman which has always had an attraction for me'; and, 'her sexual instinct (is) healthy as far as it goes, but unusually weak and fastidious.'

It must be obvious that to analyse every feature of Sue's complex character (which in itself is not always consistent) would involve a re-writing of the novel: much of the material is already to be found in our discussion of the Major Themes, which will not be repeated here. But some other essential features merit comment. Perhaps, firstly, it is best to realize that Sue is not the type of 'New Woman' of the latter end of the nineteenth century, as many critics urge. She is quite clearly a passionate disciple of the principles of Auguste Comte (1798–1857), summed up mainly in his *Positive Philosophy*, a work which J. S. Mill, one of Sue's favourite authors (and Mill himself held and promoted unconventional attitudes towards society, politics and religion) had translated and abridged in the 1850s.

Comte's views included the notion that the history of religion was 'fetishist' – i.e. that it rested on primitive, idol-like worship and crude unthinking belief – a term Sue uses of Christminster: he also asserted that institutional education was anti-intellectual. The essence of Positivism was that it rejected all speculation beyond the actually known and physically knowable. What mattered was a 'religion of humanity': experience of the senses alone was meaningful. This style of thinking strongly engages Sue Bridehead until the tragedy of the children's deaths. Thus she was not one of the 'New Women' of a later date, say of the 1890s, by which time the 'religion' was dead and J. S. Mill considered out of date.

Sue is in no way attached to politics: she is not of the suffragette type. She does not strive for male professional qualifications or economic independence. Indeed, many of her 'epicene' ideas make her the mouthpiece of Hardy's own personal ideas. Her loss of faith is an example; her rationalism, her opposition to that 'education' as offered by the crumbling, outworn élitism of Christminster is another. So also is her belief in the new historical 'Higher' criticism of the Bible (exemplified particularly in her re-arrangement of the

New Testament on historical lines (p.172) and her views on the Song of Solomon). Restless, intellectual and unfeminine in many ways, she is still no advocate of the radical 'socialist' or of the 'women's liberation' tendencies of the 1890s and later. It is important, then, not to see her as an 'advanced' woman or a promoter of feminine equality, for this will distort one's view.

Yet one feature is distinctive whatever the date: she has pronounced 'epicene' views – not for equality, but to be accepted as a woman in her own right, quite contrary to St Paul's view of women's subjection and long historically-maintained legal restriction. Sue's is a revulsion from the Victorian version of Bismarck's three K's (*Kinder, Küche, Kirche*) – children, kitchen, Church, as being the prescribed limited circle of woman's destiny. She is not domesticated, she denies and defies the Church; and, in a way, her children are forced upon her. In fact, once the story so turns that these three become her actual fate, her children die horribly; she retreats to the Church in a form of restless penance, having become a 'domesticated' housewife totally against her essential nature.

What Sue asserts is a woman's total right to her own body, and she takes this view to what may appear to be a neurotic extreme. She wishes to escape the domination of sexual power: she has a self-confessed 'curious unconsciousness of gender' that at times makes her apparently callous and self centred. The episode of her undergraduate 'lover' (pp.167 169), and her way of recounting it, is revealing in its denial of life, a selfish mental pride and a distorted self-absorption – 'my curiosity to hunt up a new sensation always leads me into these scrapes'. Now this is confused: her motives are not really adequately explained, and the outcome is hard on her victims. She is, in fact, over-intellectualized: as with Father Time (though there is not really much evidence of it in the child as he is presented) the intellect threatens and stifles the life of feelings and emotions almost to the point of becoming dehumanized. She is, alas, the victim of her over-critical intelligence and is, surely, the last person with whom Jude (or any other man) could have had a happy co-existence. A 'Hardeian' fate ruled otherwise.

Apart from her fastidious revulsion from physical sex, which makes her a curiosity outside a convent, Sue has an otherwise clear-sighted 'Positivist' view of Victorian and institutional hypocrisy. The granting of a licence in or out of church does not promote or provoke true and lasting affection; the medievalism and élitism of the Church and University system is exclusive and undemocratic; she is not deceived by robes and furred gowns, cults or traditional ritual.

She is in fact shown as something of a paradox, doubtless deliberately. On the one hand one can admire her stand as a feminist 'bachelor girl', intellectual by nature and rebelling against an entrenched, male-dominated traditional exclusiveness in society, especially through the 'upper class' who seem determined to keep the 'lower classes' in their inferior place. On the other hand, she herself tends to be flighty, inconsistent with herself, first rejecting and then accepting Jude, marrying Phillotson almost in revenge for Jude's earlier connection with Arabella (a neo-pagan working in a Church art-shop). Certainly, Sue is Hardy's first, and last, unpredictable woman: perhaps this very facet of variability and inconsistency makes her avoid true experience: she cannot herself grasp the complications of 'that mystery, her heart'.

This, of course, makes her role and destiny poignant and moving. She is part of the 'ache of modernism', a pioneer of the new urban element in an era of painful change. She has educated herself out of her class and region: but, by chance, her struggles have led to the poverty-haunted union of a non-marriage; her loss of professional status and independence; her mothering of another's child, who murders her own family: little wonder she turns back on herself, believing so passionately that life should have something more and better to offer; that the fault lies within, even if it means a painful reversal of deeply-felt and long-nurtured principles. Yet, again, one must emphasize the paradox in Sue's nature: attractive and vibrant, yet sometimes totally selfish and self absorbed; clever, well-read and perceptive, but lacking the force and power to take her destiny into her own hands. Life's bitterness and tragedy do not, in fact, enlarge her views: they rather narrow them into a morbid, almost sentimental, religious fervour. She hurts her every contact: her under-graduate friend dies, apparently, through her callousness; Phillotson is led into disgrace and degradation; Jude, whether he so deserves or not (or is it the curse of the Fawleys?) finds little happiness and much wretchedness at her hands. Her eventual rejection and desertion of him leaves him a doom-laden, tragic figure.

In her own day (that is, in Hardy's time, for it is his sole novel with a contemporary setting) Sue would be exceptional in her scepticism and in her clear rejection of the smug complacency of Browning's attitude: 'God's in His heaven – all's right with the world' – that everything is coherent, finally organized, with its social, economic, rank and status levels fixed and hardened by custom and tradition. She is a free spirit, scornful of outworn beliefs and practice. But she is a victim of her own intelligence: she will not commit herself: she fights off the inevitable compromise of society's interdependence. Perhaps she thinks overmuch of the 'social mix' and its origins and destiny, but grossly underestimates its power, strengths, and cruelties. She has become alienated; and the deaths of her children, combined with crushing poverty, break her. She is totally defeated; she turns to a religion which she intellectually despises and to a husband whom she physically loathes, as a sacrifice and a penance. Arabella's last words in the novel, surely, ring terribly true. Alive, Sue will never have peace of mind. She is at once the strongest and the strangest of all Hardy's creations, a key character, and she remains both puzzling and haunting. Her psychological dimensions lead directly to the women (cast in not so different a setting as one would imagine) of the early novels of D. H. Lawrence.

Little Father Time
'I wish I hadn't been born!'

Little Father Time presents a tangle of problems. Some part of his origins must surely be derived from Hardy's prolonged broodings over his own ancestry: there were many 'skeletons in the family cupboard' of children born out of wedlock, of overhasty marriages, and of premature births and deaths. Then, too, there is Hardy's strong pervading sense of fatalism, derived from his boyhood initiation into the manifold tragedies of human and animal life: that so many wishes are futile; that death is the inevitable end of all; that Nature is cruel. In earlier novels there is the characteristic Hardy touch of a wild so-called 'Gothic' imagination, which often threw probability and credulity to the winds to gain an extraordinary effect of macabre horror and sinister power: and with little Time he perhaps takes it to an extreme, with the child's 'quaint and weird face' like a tragic mask, his curious language and detachment, and his frightful involvement.

More factually, Little Father Time carries a reminiscence of Hardy's close friend Horace Moule (see Notes, p.23) whose suicide by cutting his throat devastated Hardy. This brilliant Cambridge scholar had a bastard child by a Dorchester girl; the boy was brought up in Australia, and was hanged there for some unspecified crime. The parallels are too strong to be ignored.

Obviously, the child is to some extent symbolic: his very name, recalling the personification of Time as an aged man, carrying a scythe and an hour-glass (the image dates from the sixteenth century) reminds us of human mortality, and that eventually all is reduced to nothing. But symbols as such cannot murder and commit suicide – as in what must be the most brutal and harrowing scene of all Hardy's fiction, or perhaps anywhere in the English novel. Of course, at this point of the story, Hardy, with his mind fixed on the ending, had to create a device to propel the final catastrophe: he had to make credible the spiritual death of Sue and her 'conversion', and the physical death of Jude as a totally broken man. This is what the disturbing scene, of tragic dimensions, actually accomplishes: it inevitably and radically 'manages' the long-doomed pair towards their extinction. It is as if the unnamed children existed merely to be killed off.

But why through this abnormal, prodigy-like, rather eerie child, with his portentous and gloomy comments on life? We shall never know: what we do know is that Hardy never forgot a vivid impression – some childhood scenes haunted his mind, and entered his prose and verse, decades after they had occurred. We know, too, from his poem 'Midnight on the Great Western' how he described what must have been an intense personal experience of a 'journeying boy', with 'listless form and face'

> Bewrapt past knowing to what he was going
> Or whence he came.

He, too, had his ticket in his hat-band (Part 5, Chapter 3, p.294) and a string around his neck for the key to his box, all in the 'lamp's sad beams'. A known and named child, or a chance experience? The symbolic value, then, and the lad's possible origins, may be debatable, but his force and character are not.

In some measure, he is made to bear out the doctor's reflection (p.356) that he was a forerunner of a new generation of children who would mirror some of the agony of social change: the notion of 'the coming universal wish not to live' is an echo of the philosophy of Schopenhauer and Hartmann. If we consider Father Time's parentage; the environment in which he must have been brought up; the actual poverty; the rootlessness; and the emotional disturbance that a sensitive child would suffer in such hostile circumstances, Little Time seems less of a mystery. Naturally, he becomes Hardy's mouthpiece for his views on the world's ways, with the tragedy of its heartlessness, especially towards the poor, the weak and the vulnerable. Like Drusilla Fawley and the widow Edlin, there is something of the 'Greek chorus' element about him: a reminder of the foreboding background in which he is cast only to be uprooted and moved around, in a poor isolated group battling for survival against life's apparent bitterness.

Nevertheless, there is still something wrong. Although his entry into the story is magnificently drawn in restrained but highly evocative prose (Part 5, Chapter 3, pp.294–6) and his departure is macabre and horrifying (p.355), during his short life with his father and Sue, Little Time does not seem to justify his original essence of 'Age masquerading as Juvenility', of seeing life and lives as whole and rounded, with some philosophical awareness of the futility and melancholy at the heart of things. He shows no interest in the active and bustling Wessex Show at which his father and Sue are (at last, and only temporarily) so happy. He comments gloomily on the inevitable withering of the beautiful pavilion of flowers; surely a child so supposedly sensitive and wise would appreciate such beauty and reflect that nature annually renews itself, endlessly and in variety, in glorious colour and sweetness – he looks and sees too close, scarcely beyond himself. Note how intense he is (p.327) at Sue's exclamation, 'O why should Nature's law be mutual butchery!': but in fact Sue has freed the birds that were meant to die. Normal death is natural and inevitable: only a quite distorted view would take this with such melancholy as to wish to invite or promote premature death.

Again, one would expect a lad of his age to be more aware of the natural processes of birth than he appears to be

(Part 6, Chapter 2, p.353); he appears ignorant where he should be understanding, and emotionally childish when he should prove his maturity. Despite the nature, level and style of Jude's and Sue's regular daily conversation, which one can never imagine being banal or crude, the child has 'learned to use the Wessex tongue', which is often ungrammatical and rough (e.g. 'No room for us, and father a-forced to go away, and we turned out tomorrow; and yet you be going to have another of us soon!'). He lacks understanding: his emotional maturity seems stunted, even distorted, for he is clearly impulsive and violent, even irrational. It could well be argued (though one must not take this too far) that in presenting this 'philosopher', Hardy is cynically attacking abstract philosophy itself, which, by thinking overmuch discounts emotions and a fundamental awareness of reality. Certainly it helps to render the child unbelievable.

But not quite. The annals of the poor, the struggling, the ill-educated, the weak and hungry, are necessarily and inevitably short and sparse. In our own more liberal day with widespread social and welfare systems, much of this misery is located, assisted and even resolved. But much human wretchedness remains: there is still social unrest and injustice. More and more instances of baby-, child-, and wife-beating are recorded. Many still hover below the subsistence-line, and the 'poverty gap' is wide. There is still considerable adult illiteracy, and divorces and broken families cause untold grief, even tragedy. The products of this kind of wretched background can be found today, especially among schoolchildren, and particularly in our urban centres. They are restless, confused, sometimes turbulent and violent, understanding neither themselves nor their apparently hostile and thwarting environment. 'Done because we are too menny' remains a haunting cry of desperate anxiety provoked by a savage grinding poverty and the remorseless hypocrisy of a selfish 'society'. It is a truism that such 'problem children' exist and persist

even in our enlightened age. Little Father Time seems, so
sadly, to foreshadow them.

Richard Phillotson

'I am a bachelor by nature . . .'

Tryphena Sparks (see Note p.46) apparently once told Hardy
of a middle-aged Berkshire schoolmaster from a village near
Fawley who came to teach in Dorset: thus some points may
be based on a bachelor Mr Holmes, schoolmaster of Athel-
hampton in Dorset, under whom she had herself worked.
According to her account, he ran into some unspecified trouble
in his fifties.

In the novel, Phillotson has an obviously crucial function
at the heart of its structure; but as a personality, he is an
interesting, though rather dull, fellow. In common with Jude
he has high initial aspirations, first for a university education
leading to a degree, and then to enter the Church, even as
a mere licentiate priest. But, unlike Jude, he is physically inert,
unprepossessing and unromantic: his desires, such as they are,
burn slow and smoulder fitfully, rather than burst into Jude's
inflamed passions.

True, he first sows the seeds of Jude's scholastic aspirations
(pp.28–31). While the rest of the Marygreen villagers 'seemed
sorry' the schoolmaster was leaving (the rector, his immediate
superior, actually absents himself deliberately), it is the small
boy Jude, aged 11, who has tears in his eyes. While he fusses
over a piano he will never learn to play, the schoolmaster
talks to the boy about intellectual and professional escape.
He gives Jude a book as a parting gift, and later sends him
others. He says he will never forget Jude, and invites the boy
to look him up if ever he visits Christminster. Yet, after the
lapse of eight years Phillotson is still a village schoolmaster
– thin, careworn, his hopes already disappointed – and he
is the first character to set the theme of failure, loneliness and

relative poverty that runs through the novel. At the age of forty-five he appears spare, thoughtful, worn and stooping, with few ambitions left (Part 2, Chapter 4, pp.121–2).

The intervention of Sue Bridehead changes all this. Twenty years older than Sue, hitherto having achieved little and felt no romantic stirrings, Phillotson is quickened, enlivened by her capricious waywardness and obviously fresh intelligence. He feels protective (pp.127–9); each has the other's photograph; he has a late spurt of ambition and is inspired with the practical if unromantic notion that if he can win her in marriage they can together maintain a larger school, achieve a greater measure of financial independence, and gain in social status. He pursues his restrained suit, sometimes with a pathetic devotion (e.g. Part 3, Chapter 6, pp.180–2), and wins – regrettably for every feeling character in the novel.

It must be said that Phillotson, during his first marriage to the mercurial Sue, behaves with extraordinary patience and self-control. He has achieved the headship and status he so long desired, but few other creature-comforts. Yet he retains a dignity, despite a schoolmasterly pettiness over detail, throughout his emotional trials; one feels some sympathy for him as Sue's aversion to his physical nearness becomes increasingly strong. He behaves with principle and dignity over the divorce: he suffers acutely as a result – he loses his more lucrative post and his sense of stability: he is brought down through shame into a self-dependence hard for an ageing man on a quarter of his old salary. He has to uproot himself, to return – a symbolic touch this – to the Marygreen whence he had first moved towards lofty goals. He is tortured, yet forgiving, even later on his bizarre re-marriage: yet Sue's eventual physical submission is spiritual death to her, and can scarcely be considered a physical triumph for him.

There is something amiss with Phillotson. Apart from his natural wish to restore his broken fortunes – and even practise a little deceit in what is, after all, a harsh and cruel world

(Part 6, Chapter 4, pp.378–9) – there is something un-
attractive about him. In common with the other characters,
he never reaches his full potential; is beaten by the world's
hypocrisy; harassed by its narrow-mindedness and its institutions. Like them, too, he is beaten by fate; uprooted and
badgered through his own goodness and sense of fitness. But
no one (excepting his old school-friend Gillingham) likes him.
At times we are bound to sympathize with his plight: 'What
do I care about J. S. Mill … I only want to lead a quiet
life!' (Part 4, Chapter 3, p.244); and when he and Gillingham
pack up Sue's things (p.256) and later, when Sue visits him,
in his shame and misery (pp.269–73), there is a touch of
pathos. Aunt Drusilla cannot compliment him (Part 3,
Chapter 9, p.210); Sue would prefer to leap out of a window,
and sleep with spiders rather than with him; Jude (naturally
enough) is appalled at both marriages.

It is a successful portrait: clearly Phillotson has deceived
himself utterly, seeing Sue not as she is, but as he wants to
see her: one of the elements of 'seemings' Hardy indicated
in the Preface. He has his convictions: as with the other
characters, he and his convictions are defeated by the twists
of fate. He has suffered for doing what seemed right. And
yet it is still hard to identify what must have been the specific
cause of his apparent revoltingness. Perhaps it is a bitter
reflection by Hardy, himself susceptible to feminine wit and
charm, of the hopeless folly of an old man, set in his ways,
falling late in love; and being somewhat too generous, too
tolerant, in a changing, uncompromising, uncomprehending
society.

Miss Drusilla Fawley

'… who spoke tragically on the most trivial subject'

and

Mrs Edlin

'Times have changed since then!'

Apart from a few casual, often un-named and uninvolved characters, Miss Drusilla Fawley, Jude's great-aunt, and her Marygreen neighbour Mrs Edlin are the only two relics of Hardy's 'rustic chorus' of the Wessex novels. They remain choric figures in the classical sense, in that they recur throughout the novel, offering background information and commenting on incidents, detached in a sense from the mainstream of the novel, but offering material not otherwise readily or (without damaging the structure) easily available. Druisilla is generally harsh and caustic, with the crusty rough tongue often a privilege of greater age, but in fact kinder than she appears: Mrs Edlin is always kindly and attentive, but can at times speak her mind with candour. Drusilla is hustled into her grave, in the 'new' part of the cemetery, with indecent haste (Part 4, Chapter 2, pp.229–30) never having married nor moved from her village limitations; Mrs Edlin, however, moves about in attendance: upon Drusilla; the weddings; Sue's third pregnancy; and is present at Jude's final illness and funeral. Both are of the stock – the working-class peasant stock of all the major characters of the novel, and of Hardy himself – and are a mine of background information and legend of an earlier, more stable era. Neither can claim a specific prototype: these would be the kinds of people Hardy sprang from, was born among, and lived with during his most impressionable years: they were part of him and of his thinking.

Drusilla is a tough old girl, full of macabre tales about the Fawley family's marriage curse: it is from her that the theme of this apparent hereditary incompatibility stems: 'There's sommat in our blood that won't take kindly to the notion of being bound to do what we do readily enough if not bound' – almost a summary of the complex natures of Jude and Sue. She is important as a focal point of messages and visits, especially when she is unwell, and as a commentator on the marriage theme in general. She has pointed views about Christminster folk, Arabella and Phillotson, and Jude's dismal folly. At times she broods in the background as an almost Cassandra-like, Meg Merrilies-type figure of the foreboding prophetess. In function, however, she is especially important because of her dwelling on particular details of the family's past, about which she remains the sole surviving source of information.

Mrs Edlin's contributions are more general and homely, and, as the survivor, can continue the choric thread until it is eventually broken by the physical death of Jude and the spiritual death of Sue. Again, like Drusilla, she can transmit messages, and as 'the only person remaining on earth who was associated with his early life at Marygreen' is invited to Jude's intended wedding, for which she brings some practical gifts. She too has a grim tale of the family's past history (Part 5, Chapter 4, p.301); has pertinent views on the difference between old- and new-style marriages, and is wary of the 'new notions'. In her day, marriages were not to be feared: the greatest dread was the death of a man – the breadwinner – in war; or actual hunger. Supposing her age to be about eighty, she would have heard her parents talk of the Napoleonic Wars at first hand, would have been a child during the American War of Independence, and would have known many village men go off to fight in various 'colonial' wars. Marriage to her was an accepted convention, entered into with as much (or as little) profound thought as is needed for a child's game.

Moving about, she helps Jude and Sue through their impoverished days at Kennetbridge, and is with Jude as his fatal illness develops. She is back at Marygreen for Sue's marriage: note how she expostulates with Sue, in her most significant dialogue (pp.384–5). This is interesting: she steps out of convention in asserting that which Sue previously has always affirmed, that love is more important than formality: the spirit more valid than the letter. And she is bold enough to tell Phillotson this to his face. The encounter (pp.386–7) is worth noting. She refuses to assist at the ceremony, and may well be the lone voice wryly re-echoing the preacher's words. She is there when Sue decides to submit to Phillotson, and laments, 'Weddings be funerals . . . Times have changed' since her own marriage over half-a-century before. She is present at the last days of Jude: at his death, alone but for the dignified corpse and the dry-eyed Arabella, she weeps quietly. Here stand the two generations, the one reflecting a traditional continuity in a stable, calm, secure, community-spirited past, the other, the more grasping urges of our own tense society; perpetually in turmoil, caught in 'the modern vice of unrest.'

Arabella Donn
'Poor folks must live!'

Arabella is supposed to have been based, physically at least, on one Rachel Hurst, a Stinsford village beauty: notable features were 'her rich colour and vanity, frailty, and artificial dimple-making'. So far as can be ascertained, Hardy made no specific references to her (apart from obvious general ones in his Preface and Postscript); but some words are worth noting from one of the very few magazine articles Hardy ever wrote, 'Candour in English Fiction': 'Life being a physiological fact, its honest portrayal must be largely concerned with, for one thing, the relations of the sexes.' It is Arabella who introduces this theme into the novel.

It is tempting, but too facile, to see Arabella solely as a stark contrast to Sue Bridehead – the flesh as opposed to the spirit; reflecting, respectively, the lower and higher aspects of Jude's nature; the *Venus Pandemos* rather than the *Venus Urania* (earthly as opposed to heavenly love, Part 3, Chapter 6, p.188): earth to Sue's fire. In Jude's thoughts, she may 'not be worth a great deal as a specimen of womankind': she has been described as the only odious woman in all Hardy's work. Certainly the animal symbolism of the pig is constantly associated with her, from the pizzle which brings Jude back to earth from his academic dreams, to her father's pork and sausage shop in the Christminster slums – the base from which she organizes the grotesque black comedy of the remarriage. Her obvious sexual desires, and her long connection with drink, reinforce the Samson and Delilah symbol in the dreary Alfredston inn wherein Arabella is instantly recognized as 'low' company – but she is triumphant there, knowing that 'she is winning her game' (p.66): Jude is to be deceived and brought down to her level, like the biblical hero, by sexual wallowing and deceit.

All this is true: but it is not the whole truth. Arabella is not so limited. She may be predictable, but she has more insight, more human (though perhaps not humane) attributes – which are wholly praiseworthy and clearly understandable – than the persistent 'low' and animal imagery would seem to support. Of course, in the structure of the novel she is needed as a foil to Sue Bridehead, and must remain the persistent obstacle, however much contrived are her coincidental arrivals and departures and chance encounters, in the quartet of conflicting characters. She is very tightly woven into the fabric of the novel, and has her own down-to-earth values: there is nothing ethereal about this 'complete and substantial female animal', and she wants a man. It may be 'only a bit of fun' for the naive Jude, but Arabella has been stirred to genuine thoughts of love and marriage (p.69). It is not mere lust, at least not on her part – 'He's the sort of man I long for'.

Of course she needs to trap him – he has the makings of a good catch – but until goaded on by her friends and 'Physician' Vilbert, Arabella is curiously ignorant of the obvious device that will suit her purpose. Jude's cooler thoughts about her as a poor specimen are belated: he obviously has other thoughts at warmer moments. For her part, she has a husband with 'earning power' to buy her 'frocks and hats', who, she thinks, will soon learn to 'stick to his trade' and abandon 'those stupid books' for more practical undertakings. She has judged her man badly; but this is not to say that, practically speaking, she is wrong: Jude gets much the same advice from a College Master. Arabella is in fact proud of him, and claims that she has not tricked him into marriage (p.80): she is sure that he will 'shake down – men always do': after all, 'married is married'. She is naturally irritated at Jude's lack of independence – he is still an apprentice – and by his academic pretensions, however many books he has had to sell to buy saucepans. But it must be asked: how far is she wrong when she believes, eventually, that she would be better off without this 'slow old coach' who has no prospect 'of ever bettering himself'? While Jude fails at Christminster, Arabella's family fails in Australia: in the same inn, now extensively modernized to suit the changing times, where Jude had drunkenly recited the Creed and changed the course of his aspirations, Arabella bounces back, full of life and earthy vigour. It is only Jude's view that she has 'no more sympathy than a tigress with his relations or him', and he certainly does not avoid spending the night with her at Aldbrickham.

Arabella then intervenes at crucial moments, either as a significant background reminder of Jude's initial folly (e.g. Part 4, Chapter 2), or dominantly as a presence and irritant (e.g. Part 5, Chapter 2): but she is never insulting to Sue, only perceptive, and her letter (Part 5, Chapter 3) about her and Jude's child, and his actual arrival, set the story on its tragic final course. She is not unkind to the child: she protests (and one can believe in) her honesty about Time's parentage and her own fidelity, and it is clear that she thinks the boy's chances in life would be better handled outside the kind of life she expects to lead henceforth.

Part 5, Chapter 5 is important: Arabella accurately gauges

the relationship of Jude and Sue, and in Chapters 7 and 8 penetrates Sue's curiously lofty attitude. Her widow's conversion to religion is short-lived: she is stirred by memories and jealousy, and becomes intent upon reclaiming Jude, her original lover. Her reactions to the tragedy of the children's deaths is as tactful and articulate as she can manage: and while Jude and Sue continue to torture themselves, Arabella takes her moment to recapture him. Had she not, Jude might have been totally abandoned. She is affectionate towards him, and certainly enjoys plotting the parody of the remarriage. But it is not entirely in a spirit of malevolent jest: once again, for better or for worse, she has a husband. Regrettably for all, she has made a bad bargain. Jude is a sick man, and she recognizes that she will have to help him, even 'support an invalid husband' by going back, how symbolically, to making blackpot and sausages, and hawking them round the streets. She knows at once that Jude's visit to Sue – which she might have prevented – has fatally undermined his precarious health: but she is practical, wants to get him home to a warm drink. She sees no phantoms during that haunting walk, or ever, but recognizes in Vilbert the next stage of her life: 'Weak women must provide for a rainy day . . . one must take the old if one can't get the young'. In this setting Jude dies: Arabella moves out into the living world, and is given the final, and searingly true, sentiment of the entire novel.

The foregoing estimate suggests that Hardy does not present Arabella (to the closely attentive reader) as a merely lustful, heartless animal, but rather as a representative of the 'new woman', physically and morally; just as Sue Bridehead is another 'new' woman intellectually and rationally. Arabella's ideas are basic and limited: a husband is, or should be, a breadwinner, and she seeks security, as everyone does, especially in a disorientated society. Her background is that of the too slowly changing village community of 'Wessex' tradition, which even the little boy Jude felt was ugly. Slowly but surely the railway, the omnibus, the redbrick suburbs are spreading the slow breakdown of timeworn convention.

Arabella has her own ambitions; above all she wants to rise in the world, and her 'education' cannot be bookish, so she uses her only talents – her body, and her mind with its fair ration of peasant cunning. She must survive: that is her aim. this raw country girl is infinitely adaptable, working to free herself from the limiting shackles of her class and status – always the most insecure and endangered class, who generally live and die at, or a little below the subsistence level. She is practical, realistic: if she does not get on, she will go under; hence her bouncing determination and vitality. Far more than the 'intellectual' Jude and Sue, Arabella pursues life, meeting and challenging the demands of the new age: she realizes, sooner and more realistically than they, that to get on one must be a little ruthless, an opportunist, a 'pusher', a promoter of oneself. It is surely a wrench of Hardeian irony that the graceless, unintellectual, pragmatic Arabella *lives*.

Summaries of chapters and textual notes

Title page

'The letter killeth' From 2 Corinthians, 3, 6: '. . . the letter killeth, but the spirit giveth life'.

Preface to First Edition

death of a woman Probably Tryphena Sparks, Hardy's cousin.
Harper's Magazine American literary magazine, founded in 1850.
matter of a title Originally the novel was entitled 'The Simpletons'; it was published in *Harper's Magazine* under the title 'Hearts Insurgent'.

Postscript (dated 1912)

a fantastic tale Hardy's *The Well-Beloved*, first serialized in 1892 and published in book form in 1897.
burnt by a bishop W. W. How, Bishop of Wakefield.
lady who . . . shuddered at the book Jeannette Gilder, an American critic, who described the book as the worst she had ever read. She did, however, later request an interview with Hardy in London.
Diderot's words Diderot was a French philosophical writer and critic (1713–84) among whose many works was an immense undertaking, a seventeen-volume *Encyclopédie*. The reference here is from the section on Natural Law.
Bludyer A violently condemning book-reviewer in Thackeray's novel *Pendennis*.
Blackwood *Blackwood's Magazine*, a literary monthly of high standards, was first published in 1817; the lady referred to here was Mrs Oliphant who, in 1896, attacked the novel in its pages in an article 'The Anti-Marriage League'. A prolific writer of about a hundred books, she married – curiously enough in the light of our story – her cousin.

Part 1

Part-title page

Marygreen Hardy's name for the village of Fawley, or Fawley Magna, on the Berkshire Downs.
Esdras From 1 Esdras, 4, 26–32.

Chapter 1

Eleven-year-old Jude Fawley is among other Marygreen villagers saying good-bye to Mr Phillotson, the schoolmaster, who is leaving for Christminster and its famous university, to pursue studies so as to graduate and perhaps then enter the priesthood. He asks Jude (who has secured a place for the teacher to store his piano) to be a good kind boy, and to visit him if ever he should visit Christminster. The lad returns to his task of drawing water from the well, sad at the master's departure; a sharp reprimand from an elderly woman rouses him to the harsh realities of his young life and limited environment.

Cresscombe Hardy's name for Letcombe Bassett.
tilted A canvas cover on a cart.
Christminster Hardy's name for Oxford. More detail comes later in Parts 2 and 6.
Jude The name of the smallest of the general epistles; it is directed against a kind of false teaching: the reader is warned against immoral and licentious practices. Some of this will seem appropriate.
Miss Fawley See Note on 'Marygreen': home of a number of Hardy's ancestors.
draw-well Deep well from which the water is drawn by a bucket suspended on a rope.

harlican Dialect term of contempt: wretch, rascal.

hipped Architectural term: remember Hardy's Dorchester apprenticeship. A 'hip' is that external angle formed by the sides of a roof when the end slopes backwards instead of terminating in a gable.

Chapter 2

Jude lives with his great-aunt Drusilla Fawley, the local baker and confectioner, who talks to some villagers about the boy. We learn that he is an orphan and that he is, for his years, an avid reader (like his cousin Sue, who has not lived locally for many years). The old lady reflects on the ill-luck that marriage has brought on the family in general. Jude returns to his regular work of bird-scaring in the fields of Farmer Troutham. Reflecting on the ugliness of the place, and feeling sorry for the birds that he deprives of food, he neglects his task; and is sharply punished, scolded and dismissed by the farmer, who has come upon the scene unobserved. Jude tells his aunt of this unfair treatment: she wishes aloud that he had gone off with the schoolmaster to Christminster. Once again, the boy meditates in his childish way on the unkindness of life; but he soon forgets his troubles and goes off, enquiring from a villager the general whereabouts of the great university town. He is given a vague direction, and soon finds himself in open country.

med May, might (dialect).

mischty Mischief (dialect).

clacker Onomatopoeic word from the sound made: a bird-scarer made of two flat pieces of wood striking each other.

tassets One of a series of overlapping pieces forming a kind of skirt in plate armour.

deedy Solemn (dialect).

Job See the biblical Job, 30, 1.

journeyman As the name implies (French *jour*: a day) a hired
  day labourer.
or'nary Inferior (dialect).
sprawl Energy, initiative (dialect).

Chapter 3

The boy is alone until he notices some tilers repairing the
roof of the Brown House: he asks them where Christminster
lies. They point out the general direction from aloft, but it
is too misty to make out anything definite. Later on, when
the workmen have gone home, the boy climbs up and looks
again. After a time the sky clears, and the setting sun picks
out the distant roofs and spires of his dream-city. Some time
later he looks again at night, and marvels at the distant glow.
Some carters pass, one of whom tells him something of the
atmosphere of learning and religion to be found there. The
child is convinced that his destiny is somehow bound up
with Christminster.

Icknield Street The Icknield Way is a pre-Roman track across
  South-West England running from the Wash to Hertfordshire: it
  follows the line from the Berkshire Downs to the course of the
  River Kennet in Wiltshire.
Brown House Possibly Hardy had in mind the Red Barn, which
  was situated where the Ridge Way joined the main Wantage
  ('Alfredston') road.
freestone-work Freestone is any fine-grained sandstone (or
  limestone) that can be cut or sawn through easily.
Herne the Hunter The ghostly huntsman of legend, said to
  haunt Windsor Great Park at night. He is mentioned in *The
  Merry Wives of Windsor* and in Harrison Ainsworth's *Windsor
  Castle*.
Apollyon King of hell, and angel of the bottomless pit, featured
  by Bunyan in his *Pilgrim's Progress* as a monstrous demon.
the captain Character in a story of W. Hauff (1802–27).

Apocalyptic writer Biblically St John: the word means a
  revelation, and applies to those whose work deals with, and
  reveals, the end or future state of the world.
Nebuchadnezzar's furnace See Daniel, III for the story of
  Shadrach, Meschach and Abednego, cast in the fiery furnace by
  the Babylonian king.
Tower of Babel See Genesis XI.
nighthawk Nightjar.
lirruping Idle (dialect)
Crozier Hotel Almost certainly Hardy's name for the Mitre
  Hotel in Oxford.

Chapter 4

The same evening Jude encounters the oddly-dressed and
ever-hurrying quack-doctor known as Physician Vilbert, on
his exactly-timed rounds of the Wessex area. He asks Jude
about Christminster, and promises to give him his own old
classical grammars from his student days – in a fortnight's
time, on his next circuit of visits. But Jude must work for them
by recommending his medical wares throughout the village.
Two weeks later Jude meets him at the expected time and
place, but the quack has quite forgotten about the books, and
Jude is bitterly disappointed. Mr Phillotson has asked for his
piano to be sent on: Jude slips in a note asking for some books,
and a package arrives. Jude takes off with his treasure into
the open country, to savour the books in isolation: he quickly
discovers that the classical grammars demand exceptional and
intensive memorizing. Once again, the boy is dejected and
disconsolate, and quite alone with his troubles.

Mount Sinai Mountain (also called Horeb) upon which the
  Tables of the Law were given to Moses.
heaven lies about them Suggested by Wordsworth's ode,
  'Intimations of Immortality': 'Heaven lies about us in our
  infancy!'

Alfredston Hardy's name for Wantage, in Berkshire, 25 miles north-west of Reading: it was the birthplace of Alfred the Great, whose statue stands in the market-place.

Grimm's Law The two brothers Grimm are celebrated as collectors of fairy-tale folklore; but both were distinguished German philologists. Jakob Ludwig Karl Grimm, through his intensive researches into language, evolved the celebrated 'Law' of the consonantal changes in the principal Aryan languages.

Chapter 5

Three or four years have passed: Jude is now a growing lad of fourteen or fifteen, working as a roundsman for his great-aunt, and unceasingly pursuing his studies. He extends his reading beyond the classics, and thinks of becoming a priest. To finance such endeavours, however, he must learn a man's trade. He apprentices himself to a local stonemason, and then to a church-builder and repairer at Alfredston, where he lodges, returning to Marygreen every Saturday for the weekend. So, studying and working, he reaches the age of nineteen.

Cotters Labourers living in what we would now call 'tied cottages'.

Caesar Julius Caesar (102–44 BC) the great Roman statesman and soldier. His Commentaries on the Gallic and Civil Wars are evidence of his cultivation and literary skill.

Virgil Latin poet (70–19 BC).

Horace Roman poet (65–8 BC).

Delphin editions A series produced in France of the great classical writers in the reign of Louis XIV for the education of his son, the Dauphin.

Dido Name given by Virgil in his *Aeneid* to Elissa, founder and Queen of Carthage: she lost her lover, and burnt herself to death.

sponge Soft dough of which bread is made.

'Carmen Saeculare' Poem by Horace (see above): the first line, 'Phoebe . . . Diana' may be translated: 'O Phoebus, and Diana queen of forests'.

Clarke's Homer The texts of Homer's epic work, the *Iliad*, in Greek and Latin, translated by Samuel Clarke in the 18th century.

Ionic The most important of the three main branches of the ancient Greek language.

Griesbach's text An eighteenth-century edition of the Greek New Testament by J. J. Griesbach (1745–1812). We know that Hardy, like Jude, studied this edition and was fascinated by its style. He enjoyed the wealth of its reflections upon life; at one time, in fact, Hardy studied hard in preparation for ordination into the priesthood.

Chapter 6

Returning home one Saturday, Jude pleasurably reflects on his extensive studies so far: in the midst of this self-contemplation he is struck by a pig's pizzle thrown at him by one of a group of three village girls engaged in rinsing off various pieces of pigs' offal in a stream. One of the girls is a sturdy-looking, well-formed girl, who 'makes up' to Jude in a teasing way. Her father is the pig breeder and jobber for whom they have been working, and her name is Arabella Donn. Her femininity obviously attracts Jude physically, and they agree to meet the next day, Sunday. Jude goes off: Arabella returns to her friends, who talk of Jude's local reputation as a scholar, and how obviously gullible and susceptible he is where young women are concerned.

Iliad With the *Odyssey*, the great epic work of Homer (late 8th century BC): it is the tale of the siege of Troy, or Ilium, in twenty-four books.

Hesiod Greek poet of the 8th century BC.

Thucydides Greek historian (about 464–402 BC), especially of the Peloponnesian War.

D.D. Abbreviation for Doctor of Divinity.

Livy ... Aristophanes There is no need for detailed notes on these. They are among the great classical writers of poetry, history and drama.

Euripides ... Antoninus As in note above.

Bede Surnamed The Venerable (about 673–735): a monk, and a celebrated ecclesiastical historian.

Alma Mater A member of a college so calls the university of which he is, or was, a member: the Latin phrase means 'kindly mother'.

the characteristic part of a barrow-pig A euphemism for the 'pizzle' (penis) of a castrated pig.

chitterlings The smaller intestines of the pig (or other cattle) especially when fried for food.

Cochin hen Fowl of a breed of poultry originally from Cochin-China, now called Viet-Nam.

deedily In a meaningful manner.

in posse Latin phrase meaning 'potential'.

conjunctive orders An awkward phrase: it must mean orders to associate himself with, to join with, a woman.

dubbin Or dubbing: a grease used to soften and waterproof leather.

Chapter 7

On Sunday afternoon Jude cannot decide whether to meet Arabella or not: he had set aside this time for some specific area of study. But, again, he has made a promise which he is loath to break; and he eagerly abandons his work and leaves. He walks to Arabella's house by the piggeries; the couple walk and talk, and call at an inn in Alfredston for tea. The tea is so long in coming that they order beer, with which they are served promptly: then they walk to Arabella's home, clasped together. Arabella's parents, and some visiting neighbours, seem already to have accepted them as a courting couple, and on his walk home Jude feels himself to be a different man: somehow his studies now seem insignificant. He leaves early for work, and retraces his steps of a few hours before. Some time later Arabella and her two girl friends discuss him, and how he can be 'caught'. Jude may fall into a trap.

Samson and Delilah The picture is symbolically appropriate. In Judges, 14–16, the strong hero lusts after alien women and is brought down by the seducer and traitress Delilah.
Η ΚΑΙΝΗ ΔΙΑΘΗΚΗΚ Greek for 'The New Testament'.
Mizzle Hasten, hurry up (dialect).
Sojer Soldier (slang).

Chapter 8

One weekend, on his usual walk home, Jude comes across Arabella chasing a wayward pig: he helps in the pursuit, kissing the girl at frequent intervals. The pig escapes: the lovers part. The following day Arabella's family and a neighbour discuss Jude: he arrives to take Arabella for a walk, and they eventually return to an empty house. There is some affectionate teasing, which leads to more serious intimate love-play.

British earth-bank Bank or mound of earth used as a rampart or fortification of an early British settlement.

Chapter 9

Two months later, during which time the lovers have met frequently, Jude tells Arabella that he wishes to go away: Arabella, who has told the itinerant quack Vilbert of her experience, and has benefited from his advice, informs Jude that she is pregnant. He decides to marry her, and abandon his plans for higher learning and a professional life. He realizes that Arabella will by no means be an ideal wife; but marriage is the only honourable course open to him. So they marry: his great-aunt is apprehensive. The pair have to live in a meagre cottage. Jude discovers that Arabella's pretty hair was a wig, and that she had at one time been a bar-attendant at Aldbrickham. But a more painful discovery is yet to come: Jude learns that she has married him under false pretences; she is not pregnant at all, and he feels hopelessly trapped.

Aldbrickham Hardy's name for Reading, the main city of Berkshire, on the River Kennet at its confluence with the Thames. Here many relics of a long history can be found.

gin Trap.

Chapter 10

The time has come round for the killing of their pig: Jude has to leave early to get to his work, but the weather – it is snowing – may prevent Challow, the local pig-sticker, from arriving, so they prepare to do the unpleasant task themselves. Jude is over-anxious, hurried, and basically unwilling to destroy life. He does the deed inexpertly, even inadvertently spilling the caught blood: the pig dies after horrible convulsions. Challow has come up unobserved, and finishes off the work, but Jude is troubled by the whole experience, and even more so when he overhears Arabella's friends openly discussing her ruse to entrap the naive and unwary bachelor. On his return home he confronts Arabella with her guile, but she remains defiant.

blackpot Black pudding, a sausage made of blood and suet.

Chapter 11

The following (Sunday) morning Arabella renews her bitterness towards Jude, and throws aside with her pig-stained hands some of his precious books: she even makes a public spectacle of herself to passing church-goers, as a battered and downtrodden wife. Jude realizes that there is no basis for this marriage. In conversation with his aunt, later on, he discovers that his own parents had parted after a bitter quarrel; in fact, his mother had then drowned herself, and the father had gone off with the boy to live elsewhere. Much the same had happened with his father's sister – 'The Fawleys were not made for wedlock.' Jude leaves for home: on his way, he deliberately treads and then jumps hard on the ice of a frozen pond: it cracks, but does not give way. He wonders what is to be done: he could get drunk, of course. He visits the inn where he had been with Arabella, and returns home, somewhat unsteady. But the house is empty: a note from Arabella informs him that she is not returning. Later, a letter arrives to tell him that she is accompanying her parents, who are emigrating to Australia, where prospects may be better. He goes into lodgings, buys his own photograph from the auction of his father-in-law's abandoned property, and burns it, frame and all. He is again alone. He walks to the spot where he first saw the glow of distant Christminster, and where he had cut his initials into a fingerpost pointing in its direction. He resolves to go to Christminster, and start afresh to fulfil his earlier scholastic ambitions.

scallops Dialect term for stringy fat, which cannot be reduced down to make lard.

pig-jobbing A small-scale commercial undertaking dealing with pigs.

Spinoza Baruch (Benedictus) Spinoza (1632–77), Jewish–Dutch philosopher, a founder of the historical explanation (sometimes called the higher criticism) of the Bible.

Part 2

Part Title

Christminster Hardy's name for the University town of Oxford,
undoubtedly because of its Christ Church, first called Cardinal
College as it was begun by Cardinal Wolsey in 1525.

Swinburne The quotations is from one of A. C. Swinburne's
poems in his collection *Songs Before Sunrise*.

Ovid Latin poet (43 BC–about AD 17). The line is from Book 4 of
his *Metamorphoses*, and can be translated, 'Living so near each
other, they became acquaintances, then friends; in course of time
love grew between them.'

Chapter 1

Three years after Jude's separation from Arabella, he walks
towards Christminster: he is now a bearded, serious-looking
young man with some all-round experience of masonry work.
He reaches the university city at night, takes lodgings, and
then walks round, ruminating and reflecting on the ghosts
of the great men of the past who seem to haunt its ancient
and learned precincts. The following day he reminds himself
of his cousin Sue and his old schoolmaster, both of whom
he believes are living here.

Dick Whittington Sir Richard Whittington (about 1358–1423)
walked to London and eventually prospered, to become 'Thrice
Lord Mayor of London': a hero of the self-made man and of
pantomime story.

'Beersheba' Hardy's name for the Oxford district known as
Jericho.

A bell began clanging A huge bell weighing seven tons in Tom
Gate Tower (the great gate of Christ Church, Oxford): it is tolled
as a curfew 101 times at five past nine.

poets abroad The allusions here are respectively to Ben Jonson
(1572–1637); Robert Browning (1812–89); and to A. C.
Swinburne (1837–1909) of Balliol College, Oxford.

the well-known three These were J. H. Newman (1801–90),
J. Keble (1792–1866) and E. Pusey (1800–82). These and others
were involved in compiling the 'Tracts for the Times', published
at Oxford between 1833 and 1841. The purpose of these
'Tractarians' as they were called, was to arrest, 'the advance of
Liberalism in religious thought'. Many of the Tractarians later
entered the Roman Catholic Church, and their whole effort and
enthusiasm is termed 'The Oxford Movement'.

the form in the full-bottomed wig Lord Bolingbroke
(1678–1751), statesman, parliamentarian, orator, diplomat and
political intriguer.

the smoothly shaven historian Edward Gibbon (1737–94)
went to Magdalen College, Oxford, at the age of sixteen, from
which he was expelled fourteen months later: however, after an
interlude, and inspired by the ruins of the Capitol in Rome, he
conceived the idea of writing a massive history of the *Decline and
Fall of the Roman Empire*, eventually published in a series of
volumes between 1775 and 1788, immensely comprehensive and
gracefully written. It remains a classic study.

he who ... in Latin An obscure reference: Hardy himself could
not remember to whom he had referred.

the saintly author Bishop Thomas Ken (1637–1711), one of the
fathers of hymnology: among his many fine hymns are 'Awake
my Soul and with the Sun' and 'Glory to Thee, my God, this
night'. He was at New College, Oxford.

the great itinerant preacher John Wesley (1703–91), educated
at Christ Church, Oxford, was the founder of Methodism: he
began open-air preaching in 1739 at Bristol, and delivered (it is
said) at least 40,000 sermons all over the country.

One of the spectres Matthew Arnold (1822–88): poet and
critic: his father was the famous headmaster of Rugby School. He
studied at Balliol College, and was later appointed to the chair of
poetry at Oxford. The quotation here is from the preface to his
Essays in Criticism, First Series.

'Why should we ... we die?' These two lines come from

'Twenty-fourth Sunday after Trinity', which appears in Keble's collection of religious poetry, *The Christian Year* (1827).

Chapter 22

Jude has to find work: daylight reveals this and other more hard-faced realities of actual existence, such as the pitiably worn stones of many of the college-buildings. He does not find work easily. He sends a note to his aunt asking for his cousin's photograph, which she sends, but warning him off trying to contact the young girl. Lonely and as yet unemployed Jude spends a great deal of his time walking round the colleges, noting, and envying somewhat his luckier student contemporaries. Some employment is offered, which he readily accepts. Having arranged his room as part-study, he is resolved to enter the university as a student. A further letter from his aunt provides more precise details of Sue's probable job, and he locates her in a shop selling theological books, arts and crafts. He watches her activities, and one day, while at work assisting in the hoisting of a block of stone, he suddenly finds her standing at his side – totally unaware, of course, of his presence, let alone their relationship. She affects him emotionally, but he has cause to reflect on the difficulties and barriers that separate them.

bankers Wooden or stone benches on which stone masons stand work for final trimming.

read ... digest A phrase from the Book of Common Prayer.

ogee dome Architecturally, an ogee is a moulding formed by two curves, the upper concave and the lower convex. The reference here is to the dome of Tom Tower, in Christ Church.

'For wisdom ... have it' From Ecclesiastes, 7, 12.

Evangelical A religious term of various shades of meaning, but all deriving from the evangel or Bible. In this early Victorian period of which Hardy speaks, it refers to the 'Low Church', whose beliefs include the justification of sinners by faith and the divine inspiration of Holy Scripture – but also in the right of individual believers to interpret scriptural passages according to their judgement.

Alleluia The same as hallelujah, the exclamation 'Praise Jehovah'.

Old-time Street Hardy's name for Oriel Street, wherein stands Oriel College.

Chapter 3

The following Sunday Jude awaits Sue's presence at the Cathedral-church: but when she arrives he does not then wish to introduce himself. A little time before this, Sue, on one of her half-day holidays, has walked out into the countryside and bought from a pedlar two statuettes of pagan deities, Venus and Apollo: furtively, almost stealthily, she manages to get them back to her room. She lies to her landlady (who is also one of the partners owning the shop) about their identity. She settles down to read from her copy of Gibbon's history, and after a while sleeps fitfully. Not very far away Jude is working at his classical texts, and reciting aloud some of the Greek Bible.

Cardinal College Hardy's name for Christ Church, Oxford.

In quo corriget Latin version of the first part of the line quoted.

dew of Hermon The river Jordan. See Psalm 133, 5, 3.

Cyprus Third largest island in the Mediterranean, of great antiquity. The island was famous for the worship of Venus.

Galilee Area of Palestine (now part of Israel) prominent in the gospel stories of Christ's ministry.

St Silas This is based on the church of St Barnabas, Oxford.

the Christian Year See Note (Part 2, Chapter 1) on 'Why should we . . . we die?'

Julian the Apostate Roman emperor (331–63): he secretly abandoned Christianity and attempted to restore paganism. He was killed during a battle in his invasion of Persia, and is

supposed to have cried out before death 'Thou has conquered, O
Galilean' ('Vicisti Galilae').

'Thou hast ... thy breath!' From Swinburne's 'Hymn to
Proserpine'.

Latin cross An upright cross with the lowest limb longest.

'*All hemin ... di autou!*' This is from the Greek version of 1
Corinthians: 'But to us there is but one God, the father, of whom
all things, and we in him, and one Lord Jesus Christ, by whom
are all things, and we by him.'

Chapter 4

One day Jude was working inside a church when Sue and
her elderly companion came in to worship: the young girl
arouses his amorous feelings, but he recognizes his impossible
situation. Sue Bridehead, however, calls in at the stone-
mason's yard: she had learned by chance of her cousin's
presence in Christminster. As it is likely that she will soon
be leaving, she wanted to see him first. He arranges a
rendezvous that same evening: at last they meet and talk
freely. She knows of Jude's old schoolmaster, Mr Phillotson,
who lives at a nearby village. They decide to walk to the
schoolhouse. Phillotson is a changed man. Now forty-five years
old, he is thin, worn, and disappointed looking. He does not
remember Jude. He has long abandoned any academic
ambitions. They talk together for a time, and then the two
cousins walk back. Jude is unhappy over Sue's likely departure, but she has violently offended her religious landlady and
cannot stay. Jude suggests that she tries to help as a pupil-
teacher, much needed by Phillotson: perhaps she will then
enrol at a teachers' training-college – he wants to keep her
near him, though this is not openly stated. Jude in fact visits
the schoolteacher the next evening to ask Phillotson if he would
consider this possibility; he agrees, and Sue herself warms
to the idea.

erotolepsy An 'attack' of strong sexual desire – the use here of this word inviting a comparison to epilepsy.

cross in the pavement This was in Broad Street, Oxford, on the spot where, on 16 October 1555, Bishops Cranmer, Latimer and Ridley were burnt for 'heresy'. In 1841, the Martyrs' Memorial in nearby St Giles was erected in their honour.

Lumsdon Hardy's name for Cumnor, then separated from Oxford by a stretch of wooded country.

Chapter 5

Sue Bridehead does well as a pupil-teacher. She lives near the master's school-house, and in the evenings, under the eye of her landlady Mrs Hawes, Phillotson gives her private lessons. He finds himself attracted to her – not passionately, but pleasurably.

One day they take their pupils to Christminster to visit an exhibition of religious items and there, by chance, they meet Jude. Both men, especially during a lively exchange set off by the religious exhibits, are sensitive to Sue's presence. Another day the dreaded school-inspector arrives unexpectedly. Sue is so scared that only Phillotson's solicitous attentions rally her round; she has, in fact, presented herself well as a pupil-teacher. Jude has been invited to walk out with them on the Friday: when he arrives he sees them together, walking close, and again feels aggrieved and helpless.

HM Inspector His (Her) Majesty's Inspector of schools: they were Civil Service officials who (at that time, much less so today) held regular inspections of teachers and the taught. They were regarded as the 'king of terrors' (p.128) because they could inspect schools without warning, and teachers' pay could depend on the standards reached by their classes.

Code Rules governing various aspects of school administration.

Jerusalem A brief collective note on the model of the Holy City: Mount Moriah, a hill on which stood Solomon's Temple; the

Valley of Jehoshaphat, between the capital and the mount of
Olives; City of Zion, Jerusalem itself, the Heavenly City sacred to
three major religions, Christian, Jewish and Muslim; the Mount
of Olives, ridge of hill to the east, the Garden of Gethsemane
lying at its foot.

Chapter 6

Jude visits his old aunt, Drusilla Fawley, now bedridden. She
talks about Sue's background. She was, Drusilla says, an
impertinent and somewhat unruly child; and she warns Jude
to steer clear of complications. A village neighbour arrives
to nurse the old lady, and adds her memories of Sue as a
sharp, pert, tomboyish child. Meeting other villagers, Jude
talks to them of the atmosphere of Christminster, and admits
to them that he has not yet achieved any academic footing
there: he thinks he needs extra directed tuition. On return
to Christminster he writes to five of the college principals;
while awaiting an answer he learns that Mr Phillotson is
moving south to a larger school, but Jude is oppressed by
a sense of failure and inadequacy. If only he had Sue for
himself he feels he could abandon his perhaps idealistic
ambitions, and yet be happy. A reply arrives: it firmly
recommends Jude to keep to his own sphere and trade – he
recognizes this as the bitter truth. He abandons his reading
to go out drinking, and begins to think of Christminster less
as an academic enclave than as a centre of active human
beings living out ordinary and normal lives: working, loving,
playing. At a public concert he feels he sees, properly for the
first time, the real people, the ordinary citizens, the real
Christminster.

'Excelsior' Poem by the American, H. W. Longfellow.
'There was a sound of revelry by night' The opening of the
  eve-of-Waterloo section of Lord Byron's poem, *Childe Harold*,
  Canto 3, line 21.

'The Raven' Grim poem by the American, E. A. Poe, from which the subsequent quotation is taken.

well-known writer This refers to Thomas Carlyle, whose *Sartor Resartus* (Book 1, Chapter 3), mentions a spinning-top in words almost identical to those Hardy uses.

genius loci The spirit of the place (Latin).

Crusoe Robinson Crusoe, in Daniel Defoe's story, built himself a boat, but it was too big and heavy to drag to the water.

'Above . . . rise!' From Götterdämmerung, by the German lyric poet H. Heine (1797–1856).

singularly built theatre The Sheldonian, the Senate House of Oxford University, designed by Wren; it is circular in shape.

great library The Bodleian Library, based on the collection of Humphrey, Duke of Gloucester (died 1447) and enlarged by the addition of Sir Thomas Bodley's library (given to him by the Earl of Essex). It is now the university library of Oxford, with a priceless collection of books and manuscripts.

T. Tetuphenay An invented name; it could be derived from a Greek word meaning 'to have beaten'.

The Fourways Junction of streets known as Carfax.

Chapter 7

Jude realizes that his academic and amorous ambitions are equally futile: depressed, he spends much of his time in a tavern, eating little but drinking much, with an assortment of Christminster citizenry. Challenged one evening to say the Creed in Latin, he does so: and then, disgusted with the blasphemy of it all (he was urged on, in drink, by several betting men) he walks off to Sue's cottage. She takes him in: he sleeps until dawn in a chair, and, waking early, slips away. Returning to his lodging he finds a note of dismissal: news of his drunken behaviour has spread quickly. He decides to move away from all the bitterness and disappointment that Christminster has represented: he returns to Marygreen. On the way he pawns his waistcoat for some ready money, and eventually reaches his aunt's home. Back in his old room he feels wretched and miserable. He recognizes his folly and weaknesses. He would like to become a licensed preacher, at least: but he needs hope to support him.

Tinker Taylor From the well-known jingle children use for counting out.

'Credo ... Amen.' For convenience, the whole of the Creed recited by Jude is here translated as one piece: 'I believe in one God, the Father almighty, Maker of heaven and earth, of all things visible and invisible ... And was crucified for us under Pontius Pilate, and was buried. And rose again on the third day, according to the Scriptures ... And in the Holy Spirit, the Lord and life-giver, Who proceeds from the Father. Who with the Father and the Son is together worshipped and together glorified. Who spoke through the Prophets. In one holy Catholic and apostolic Church. We confess one Baptism to the remission of sins. And look forward to the Resurrection of the dead. And the life of the world to come. Amen.'

Nicene The only creed of the church which has received total sanction, so called from the Council of Nicaea in AD 325 when it was originally drawn up: there have since been re-affirmations and some additions.

the Ratcatcher's Daughter Popular ballad of Victorian beer- and music-halls.

Laocoön Celebrated sculpture group, now in the Vatican museum: it shows Laocoön (a priest who angered Apollo) and his two sons being crushed by two huge serpents coiled about their limbs. The expressions of fear and agony are striking.

Part 3

Part Title

Melchester Hardy's name for Salisbury, on the River Avon in Wiltshire, with a fine Early English Cathedral whose origins date from the thirteenth century. There are numerous old monuments and historic buildings.

Sappho From a poem in H. T. Wharton's *Sappho* (1885).

Chapter 1

The more Jude thinks of the life and work of the licensed preacher, the more he feels it to be his destiny. He does nothing to promote this move, however, and for a time does casual local work in stone. His hopes revive when Sue visits him. She intends to enrol at a teacher-training college in Melchester: there is a theological college there, too. Surely he could work at his trade and save, so that he could eventually take a course there. Later in the New Year Sue writes: she is unhappy at college. She has no friends and she asks Jude to visit her. He goes there and finds her subdued, self-disciplined. He talks to her of Phillotson, and Sue tells him that when she leaves the college she is to marry the schoolmaster and set up a mixed school somewhere. Again Jude feels dejected and disconsolate, but he finds some work and settles down to read. He hires a harmonium, the better to practise church music.

days of his vanity See Ecclesiastes 9, 9.

temperance hotel Hotel where spirituous drinks are unavailable and forbidden.

murrey-coloured Mulberry-coloured, dark purple.

Paley and Butler William Paley (1743–1805), archdeacon of
Carlisle, whose massive work, *A View of the Evidences of
Christianity* (1794), long remained a standard. Joseph Butler
(1692–1752), celebrated priest, whose great work was *The Analogy
of Religion* (1736).

Newman See Note on 'the well-known three', which also mentions
another of the Tractarians, Edward Pusey.

Chapter 2

A few weeks later Sue and Jude go on an outing: they walk
so far out into the country that they have to stop at a shep-
herd's cottage overnight. Early next morning they return to
Melchester. Sue naturally expects trouble for her absence
without permission. Jude is happy to be given a little photograph of her.

Wardour Castle Near Tisbury, Wiltshire, built by James Paine
in the eighteenth century. This 'castle' is more of a grand house:
the old castle lies in ruins.

Fonthill Probably Fonthill House, near the attractive Wiltshire
village of Fonthill Bishop.

Gothic In architecture, a style with high-pointed arches and
clustered columns, in contrast with the starker lines of classical
building.

Corinthian An ornate style of Greek architecture.

Del Sarto ... Carlo Dolci Andrea del Sarto (1488–1530),
Florentine painter; Guido Reni (1575–1642), Italian painter;
Spagnoletto (1585–1656), Spanish painter, mainly of religious
works; Sassoferrato (1605–85) (Giovanni Battista Salvi), Italian
painter, mainly of religious works and particularly famous for his
madonnas; Carlo Dolci (1616–86), Florentine painter.

Lely Sir Peter Lely (1618–80), Dutch painter who came to
England with William of Orange in 1641 and painted many
portraits of him and of Mary, his Queen; later, at the
Restoration, he dominated the Court artists by his easy style.

Reynolds Sir Joshua Reynolds (1723–92). Superb portrait
painter, appointed President of the newly founded Royal
Academy in 1768; a gifted artist and a man of culture.
chainey China (dialect).
ba'dy Bawdy, crude.
chimmer Chamber, room (dialect).
Ishmaelite An outcast, as was Ishmael, the son of Abraham and
Hagar. (See Genesis 16.)

Chapter 3

At the training college in Melchester the previous evening,
Sue's absence is noted and gossiped over: when she does return,
she is reprimanded and awarded punishment by solitary con-
finement for a week. The other students 'strike' in sympathy:
meanwhile Sue escapes, daringly and dangerously, from a
window, and has apparently waded deep through the nearby
river to make good her flight. She then appears, soaked
through and bedraggled, at Jude's lodgings. She is made to
change into Jude's suit and, a little warmed through, falls
asleep.

round robin A paper with signatures in a circle, so that no one
may seem to be ringleader.
Library of the Fathers. Work by the cleric Edward Pusey (see
Note on 'the well-known three').
Parthenon frieze The finely-sculptured panels of the most
celebrated Doric temples of Greece, on the south side of the
Acropolis at Athens. During 1801–16, most of the panels were
removed by Lord Elgin to the British Museum, London.

Chapter 4

The two cousins talk. Sue relates her experiences of an innocent love-affair, when she was eighteen, with an under-
graduate now dead. She is unconventional but untarnished,

with neither time for nor patience with the medievalism of Christminster. Jude tells her of his eager wish to become a licentiate clergyman: they argue lightly over religious hypocrisy and convictions. Again, Sue sleeps at his lodgings. Jude washes himself outside by starlight.

Lemprière . . . the Bible Little would be gained by detailing these writers of various languages and styles.

Long-Acre London street – of no special significance here.

'twitched the robe . . . draped.' From R. Browning's poem 'Too Late'.

'O ghastly . . . Gods!' From A. C. Swinburne's poem 'Hymn to Proserpine'.

brochures Pamphlets (French).

Voltairean Like (the opinions of) Voltaire (1694–1778): great French sceptic, dramatist and historian.

Solomon's Song The Canticles in the Old Testament; much of this is clearly erotic but it was included in the Bible as it could be interpreted as a 'rhapsody', or emotional, enthusiastic utterance of feeling and passion, to the greater glory and splendour of God.

epicene Common to both sexes.

Ganymedes In Greek mythology, the cup-bearer to Zeus: the classic type of youthful male beauty.

Chapter 5

When Jude returns Sue is dressed and ready to leave: she decides to go to the sister of one of her fellow students out at Shaston, at least for a time. Quietly they make their journey to the station: she warns him not to fall in love with her. A day later she writes informing him that she is comfortably lodged, and that Jude could love her if he so wished: he writes several times without provoking any response. Eventually he travels to Shaston, and finds her unwell. She cannot return to college because the rumour has been spread of their having lived together, and her reputation is thereby endangered. She is afraid that she and Jude have been too close; but she wants to remain as his dear friend, and will be returning to Melchester to collect her things. They could then enjoy again one of their walks together.

Shaston Hardy's name for Shaftesbury. See Note on title-page of Part 4.
dew-bit Picturesque phrase for light refreshment taken before breakfast.

Chapter 6

Richard Phillotson, now moved to a school at Shaston, is intent on marrying Sue Bridehead: he often reads over and over her letters to him written while she was at training-college, and looks at some photographs of her, one of which he kisses ardently. Thus he cherishes his secret dream under the cloak of schoolmasterish respectability. He goes to visit Sue at the college, and finds her gone, in some disgrace. By chance he meets Jude, and both are embarrassed, but they talk over Sue's flight and the ensuing scandal. Jude recounts the whole innocent truth, and Phillotson goes off. Later Sue appears, and Jude tells her the story of his shameful marriage. They part, having decided that for them marriage is out of the question, both being attached in some way to another: but surely, they feel, they can, as cousins, maintain a close and happy friendly relationship.

National schoolmaster Master at one of the schools organized by the National Society for Promoting the Education of the Poor in the Principles of the Established Church.
rustication Banishment (or even expulsion) from a college.
Pantheon Temple dedicated to all the gods.
Venus Urania Goddess of spiritual love.

Chapter 7

A letter from Sue to Jude announces that she is to be married to Phillotson in a few weeks: Jude is appalled, for her and for himself. She even asks him to be her 'best man' at the wedding, for she has no other willing close relation: he agrees, and suggests that Sue could be married from his house as more proper, considering their family connection. So Sue arrives, lives on a separate floor, and the wedding day comes: Jude and Sue walk out early to the church, she holding his arm. Sue and Phillotson are married: it seems that she is belatedly hesitant and anxious at the fateful step she has taken.

residence of fifteen Marriage by special licence involves one party of the marriage having been in residence, for a period of at least fifteen days, in the parish where the marriage is to take place.

Perpendicular A late English style of architecture (late 14th to mid-16th century) with such features as vertical window-tracery, fan-tracery vaulting, and panelled walls.

'...I can...womanhood!' From R. Browning's poem, 'The Worst of It'.

Chapter 8

Jude hopes that in some strange way, Sue will not stay with the schoolmaster that night – that she will return from London. But though this preys on his mind, he is brought back to reality by means of his aunt's worsening condition, also the promise of some work in Christminster. His aunt, whom he visits, is indeed ill, and he writes to Sue telling her of the situation and arranging a consequent meeting. Back in Christminster, which he now views quite differently and detachedly, he takes up his old lodgings; but he is not really sure that he wants to work there again. He has a drink with an old crony of his past, and is amazed to find Arabella there working as a barmaid, laughing and joking with customers. Jude overhears enough to gather that she has married and left a husband in Australia: then they meet, and discuss their present situation. They propose to meet after closing time to talk it over: but of course Jude has missed his train and his appointment with Sue. Telling Arabella of his aunt's illness, Jude is forced to allow Arabella to accompany him to see her.

Old-Midsummer eves Various superstitions were long
associated in Wessex (and doubtless elsewhere) with this date in
the Old Style calendar (i.e. dating from before 1752).
Aldbrickham Hardy's name for Reading. See Note on
title-page of Part 5.

Chapter 9

The married but long-separated couple return to Christ-minster and then walk towards Alfredston. Arabella tells her own story: she has married in Australia, and left her husband there. She goes into the hotel while Jude strolls about; suddenly Sue is beside him. She had gone to Alfredston, had reached Marygreen and thought that Jude had not kept their appointment because she was now married; she feared that, foolishly, he had done something dreadful. He contrasts vividly Sue and Arabella, much to the latter's disadvantage. They move off together. He does not tell her of Arabella's re-appearance. Sue seems much as she was, but Jude senses that she is unhappy. They pass the house where Jude had once lived as a newly married man, and the field where, as a boy, he was punished for his negligence. When they reach the old aunt's cottage they find that she has struggled out of bed and is sitting, wrapped up, downstairs. The old lady roundly condemns both their marriages. Later, Sue admits that she ought not to have married, and goes off. Jude receives a letter from Arabella, which tells him that her Australian husband has arrived in England and is taking up the proprietorship of a profitable tavern in South London.

She plans to return to him and wishes Jude good-bye; she hopes he will never do anything to disturb or affect her present – and now much more promising – marriage.

Chief Street Hardy's name for the High Street.

Genoa Italian city and provincial capital, 250 miles north-west of Rome. Genoa is an ancient city, with many imposing buildings and celebrated palaces.

Lazarus From the principal figure in the painting by Sebastiano del Piombo (1485–1547), in London's National Gallery. For the Biblical reference, see Luke 16.

Chapter 10

Jude returns to Melchester, and attempts earnestly to renew his studies for the priesthood. He develops his knowledge of and skill in church music, and joins a local church choir. He is much moved by a new hymn they practise, and learns that the composer is a local man. Jude imagines him to be someone who would surely understand his various difficulties, to whom he could talk freely and lay bare his soul. Discovering the composer's whereabouts, Jude makes an awkward journey to visit him. He finds the man pleasant, at least at first, but interested principally in commercial success. On his way home, rather depressed, Jude reflects on his own naiveté: arriving, he finds a letter of invitation from Sue, to dine that very day: of course he has lost that chance because of his wild-goose chase. However, he sends off a letter of explanation, and Sue replies, asking him to visit them on a particular day, as otherwise she would be at work in her husband's school. Jude goes.

'insulted . . . rights' From Gibbon's *Decline and Fall*, Chapter 15.

thorough-bass In singing, a bass part all through a piece.

Kennetbridge Hardy's name for Newbury in Berkshire, with its number of old buildings: it is said to have been the last place in England to have made use of the stocks.

Part 4

Part-title page

Shaston Hardy's name for Shaftesbury, Dorset. In fact, it is its old name and was once the ancient British Palladour. It stands on the edge of a 700 foot high plateau, with views over Blackmoor Vale (see Note below). There remain some picturesque and interesting buildings.

'Whoso ... Pharisee.' John Milton in his preface to *The Doctrine and Discipline of Divorce* (1643).

Chapter 1

Jude reaches Shaston, a picturesque historic town, a centre of pilgrimage and wayfaring commerce: he makes his way to the schoolhouse. He and Sue converse; they feel close, and she tells him that he must go away, for she is a creature of impulse and passion – she feels that Jude will suffer as a consequence. But Jude has missed the coach. He wanders about waiting for the next, and sees Sue at home, looking earnestly and thoughtfully at a photograph, whose he cannot know, but he hopes it is his. He must see her again very soon.

'From whose ... arise.' From Michael Drayton's *Poly-Olbion* (1563–1631). (See Notes on Chapter 4.)

Vale of Blackmoor (Or Blackmore – 'The Vale of the Little Dairies'). Deep alluvial valley, in a part of Dorset near which Hardy lived for two years. He mentions it frequently in his novels; it is the country of the dialect poet, William Barnes's, best poetry. (See Note on The Author.)

Old-Grove Place There is an old house in Shaftesbury called 'Grove Place'.

Apocryphal Gospels Not the poet William Cowper; B. H. Cowper's work with that title was published in 1874, and dealt

with those books accepted by neither the Christian nor the Jewish
religions as divinely inspired.

Apologetica Christian apologetics, that is, arguments defending
Christianity.

Joseph See Genesis, 37, 5.

Don Quixote Idealistic and vainly heroic character of Cervantes'
masterpiece of that name, first published in 1605.

St Stephen The first Christian martyr (died AD 33); he was
charged with preaching 'against the Temple and the Law', and
was eventually stoned by an angry crowd. See Acts 6 and 7.

Chapter 2

Sue writes to Jude, telling him not to come as invited, and he
agrees to this. He then has a letter informing him that his old
aunt is dying: he gets there, and she has already died. He
writes to Sue about their family loss, telling her of the funeral
arrangements. Sue attends the funeral; after the ceremony,
they talk over their late aunt's sombre and indeed prophetic
views about their marriages. Jude regrets his marriage; Sue,
in a guarded way, suggests that hers to the schoolmaster has
been one in ceremony only, and that she is already unhappy.
Jude then tells her of his unexpectedly renewed association
with Arabella; she then talks with bitter regret of her own
marriage. She stays the night at the widow Edlin's house.
Neither can sleep: very early in the morning the cry of a
rabbit in pain is heard – it is caught in a trap. Jude goes
out and relieves its intense agony by killing it quickly; Sue
has also heard the noise, and the two talk. Jude confesses his
love. Sue talks of the patient, shameful submission of woman
through the covenant of marriage custom and the superstition of the age, and they part.

gin A trap, net or snare.

Chapter 3

Next day Sue leaves for home. Jude accompanies her some of the way, and they part with a passionate embrace. Jude now has a new resolve, and he burns all his volumes on theology and ethics. In his love for Sue he will no longer be a hypocrite in his own eyes. Meanwhile Sue has gone on her tearful way, thinking herself weak and resolving, in her own misery, to make Jude suffer. Phillotson meets her, giving her the day's news, which includes that of the visit of a schoolmaster friend, a Mr Gillingham, who intends to call again soon. At home, Phillotson is engaged in school work – it is getting late. He finds that his wife has retreated downstairs, and he opens the door, thinking something is wrong. He cannot understand her violent, weeping opposition to his intrusion. Next day she suggests that they should live apart: she is not happy with the marriage. She feels that they can remain friends, but that she cannot allow the intimacy of marriage; she further tells him that she wishes to live with Jude. Phillotson thinks her suggestion monstrous, but their school-day has started and, in a series of notes to each other, she asks for pity, he for understanding. She wants them to live apart under the same roof, and the puzzled and misgiving Phillotson reluctantly agrees. The atmosphere is one of continuous strain.

whited sepulchre A hypocrite. See Matthew, 23, 27.

J. S. Mill's words John Stuart Mill (1806–73): philosopher and economist. He founded the Utilitarian Society and movement, the basis of whose philosophy was 'the greatest happiness of the greatest number'. Such happiness was the criterion of ethical right and wrong, and pleasure and freedom from pain the only desirable ends of life. Mill's writings had considerable influence: he himself may be regarded as the philosophical radical of the Victorian era. The quotation here is from his classic *On Liberty* (1859). It is worth noting that in this same year were published

Marx's *Criticism of Political Economy*, Darwin's *The Origin of Species by Natural Selection*, Dickens's *A Tale of Two Cities* and George Eliot's *Adam Bede*.

argumentum ad verecundiam appeal to modesty (Latin).

Humboldt In Chapter 3 ('Of Individuality, As One of the Elements of Well-being') J. S. Mill in his *On Liberty* (see Note above) quotes from a work of the German philologist and man of letters Karl Wilhelm von Humboldt (1767–1835).

Chapter 4

Phillotson, pursuing his hobby of Roman antiquities, busies himself until two o'clock in the morning. Still mentally pre-occupied, and forgetting their agreement to change rooms, he wanders thoughtlessly into Sue's bedroom. She springs up in alarm, opens the window and jumps out. Alarmed – and hurting himself in his haste to see the extent of Sue's injuries – he rushes out, to find her dazed but conscious and not really hurt. He helps her back inside and up the stairs; then, dejected and depressed, he goes to his room.

The next evening, Phillotson makes his way to the little town of Leddington, where his friend Gillingham teaches. He tells Gillingham about his wretched predicament: that he loves a wife who does not love him, and that she apparently loves another, her cousin. He tells his friend that he must let Sue go, whither she will. Gillingham suggests that he keep his wife, but Phillotson leaves for home. The next morning, he tells Sue that she can go if she so wishes; and she goes, albeit a little tearfully. Gillingham arrives, to find his friend sorrowful and deeply distressed. Together they pack the things Sue has left behind.

newel Upright post at the end or corner of a stair handrail.

'Where Duncliffe ... Away ...' From 'Shaftesbury Feair', by the Dorset dialect poet William Barnes (1801–86). See Note on The Author.

cloty Dirty. The Stour waters Blackmoor Vale.

'Where Stour . . . fed.' From *Poly-Olbion* by Michael Drayton, an immense undertaking in which the poet attempted to describe everything of antiquarian and topographical interest in Great Britain.

Leddonton Hardy's name for the little town of Gillingham.

Wintoncester Hardy's name for Winchester, the ancient capital of Wessex and England, lying on the River Itchen. The splendid medieval cathedral is the second longest in Europe, and the city contains innumerable historic sites.

lumpering Struggling, labouring.

toled Lured, enticed (dialect).

good-now Exclamation of wonder, surprise, entreaty: Hardy rendered it as the equivalent of the American 'I guess'.

Laon and Cythna Lovers in Shelley's *The Revolt of Islam* (1818).

Paul and Virginia Lovers in Bernardin de St Pierre's novel, *Paul et Virginie* (1786).

all abroad Not thinking clearly.

rummer Large drinking-glass.

rafted Very upset (dialect).

Chapter 5

Sue had written to Jude a day before, hoping that he would meet her at the station. He does so, but he has booked a room at Aldbrickham to avoid scandal: they are on affectionate terms. Jude explains that Arabella wants a valid divorce so as to clear her own marriage and this he has agreed, thus freeing himself from that ill-fated tie. Phillotson too has communicated with him, asking that Sue be loved and treated tenderly. She is, however, not yet certain that she wishes to commit herself to Jude entirely. She does not, for example, wish to share a room with him at the arranged hotel. They find lodgings elsewhere, at the George, where Jude had stayed with Arabella when they renewed their acquaintance

– a fact that Sue learns from a maidservant. This upsets her; she feels that Jude has been false to her, and they argue. When he tells her of Arabella's remarriage the two cousins are reconciled. Nevertheless, they part to go to separate rooms.

Aldbrickham See Note on Part 1, Chapter 8.

'the soldier-saints ... bliss.' From R. Browning's 'The Statue and the Bust'.

'the shadowy third' From R. Browning's 'By the Fireside'.

'... from whom ... can divide me!' See Romans, 8, 38–9.

'Epipsychidion' Long poem (about 600 lines) by P. B. Shelley (1792–1822): the second couplet (without the initial 'A') comes first in lines 21-2; the first comes later in lines 190–1. Hardy considered Shelley 'our most marvellous lyrist', enjoyed a close knowledge of his poetry and felt some kinship with his essentially Christian spirit.

Chapter 6

Back at Shaston, Phillotson is questioned about his domestic affairs by the chairman of the School Committee: he tells the bald truth of the matter. At a private meeting of the Managers, he is asked to resign for – in their words – condoning adultery. He is firm about not resigning, though his friend thinks it would be much better and less humiliating if he did. He is in fact officially dismissed, but some of Shaston's lesser citizenry and wayfarers are vocal and eventually violent on his behalf, and the master becomes ill at this ugly turn of events. Gillingham writes a letter to Sue, which she receives in a roundabout way, and she comes over to see him. She is kind and solicitous: he tells her that she can stay; he is prepared to forgive all. But she remains firm: she claims that she has been wicked, and cannot now return. The sick man assumes that she and Jude are living as man and wife; he thinks it right that he should arrange a proper separation, so that she and Jude can legally marry.

standards Levels or classes of attainment once used as categories of attainment in most pre-1948 schools.

topper The word here means a strong blow to the head.

Part 5

Aldbrickham See Note on Part First, Chapter VIII.
'Thy aerial . . . body' This quotation comes from *Thoughts of the
Emperor Marcus Antoninus Aurelius*, which was translated in 1862
by G. Long.

Chapter 1

February of the following years finds Jude and Sue living at
Aldbrickham in the same relationship: she keeps house. Her
divorce from Phillotson is now absolute, as is his from Arabella. Both are now free: they can marry one another if either
so wishes or chooses, but Sue is opposed to any such contract
from her experience and by her nature. Jude feels that she is
elusive: they drop the subject in open conversation, although
each feels strongly about its importance. Jude has a little
monumental masonry which keeps him in fairly regular, but
not very lucrative, employment.

Nemesis In Greek mythology, the goddess of retribution.

Chapter 2

At the end of February Jude returns home to hear that
Arabella has called: she calls again much later to tell him
that she (Arabella) is not after all married, and has other
troubles which she wants to explain privately and personally
to Jude alone. So Jude goes out, quite late at night, to accompany her back to her lodgings and hear what she has to say
– but Arabella is nowhere to be found. Jude feels he ought
to help her if he can: after all, he has been married to her,

and he has never been physically close to Sue, who is still evasive about marriage. She, realizing this, suggests that they should marry after all. The next morning Sue hopes that Arabella is all right: in fact she goes to the inn where she is lodging to find out. They meet; while they talk, a telegram arrives indicating that Arabella's husband-to-be does in fact now want her back, and will marry her in England to make a fresh start: Arabella suggests that it would be a good thing if Sue and Jude were also to marry. She still wants to contact Jude personally, but says that she will write to him.

oneyer Possibly (like 'oneyre' and 'oner') someone unique in some way, an individualist.

Chapter 3

Returned home, Sue tells Jude of her meeting with Arabella: she now feels even more that marriage is an institutional trap. At the moment of calling on the priest about the banns, they decide to postpone their decision over marriage, and the banns are not called. Then Arabella's promised letter arrives, with some significant news. It appears that she has now married (in fact remarried) her Mr Cartlett: more importantly, she reveals that Jude has a son by her, born in Sydney, Australia: she thinks that Jude ought to assume full responsibility for him. Jude and Sue agree, emotionally, that they should look after him, whether he is Jude's son or not; and that now they should marry, so that the child can accept them as parents. The boy arrives: he is frightened, pale, serious, unsmiling. He has walked the lonely way from the station to the house. Jude dreams of educating him, so that the boy might achieve and accomplish all that had been denied his father. Marriage now seems essential.

Via Sacra Street in ancient Rome – not 'Holy Street', but 'Street of the Oath'.

Octavia Sister of the Roman emperor Augustus. On the death of her husband, Marcellus, in 40 BC, she married Mark Antony, who swiftly deserted her for Cleopatra.

Livia (55 BC–AD 29); first the wife of Tiberius Claudius Nero, from whom she was divorced in 38 BC by command of Augustus in order that he could marry her himself.

Aspasia Athenian courtesan. In 445 BC Pericles divorced his wife and made Aspasia his mistress; such was her influence over him that some authorities insist that the Samian and Peloponnesian wars were attributable to her.

Praxiteles Athenian sculptor of the third century BC.

Phryné (*c.* 340 BC); daughter of Epicles. Another Athenian courtesan – and a famous beauty. She became the mistress of the painter Apelles, and served as a model for his 'Venus Anadyomene'.

'Can you ... love ...' Sue is quoting three lines from 'Song' by T. Campbell (1777–1844).

'Let the day ... conceived!' See Job, 3, 3.

fly One-horse hackney carriage.

Chapter 4

The next morning, the little boy is questioned: he has been nicknamed Little Father Time, for his features are old and he is serious and rather precocious. He has never been christened. Jude and Sue set in motion the procedures for their Registry Office marriage. The only one invited is the old widow Mrs Edlin, the late great-aunt's companion: she arrives with some homely gifts. They all talk together, and the old lady talks about a long-past event of local tradition, in which a possible ancestor of the cousins stole the dead body of his son, for which offence he was hanged on Brown House Hill. Sue thinks it ominous: but she and Jude go off to be married. At the last moment, Sue is upset and disturbed by

the artificiality of the scene, the unnaturalness of the circumstances and of the marriage covenant. Once again, the
decision to marry is postponed: perhaps a church wedding
would be better and less unpleasant. The old widow-woman
is amazed and perplexed at their inconsistency and inability
to make a final decision. Yet Sue considers the marriage
merely postponed: she and Jude are happy together as they
are; and that is all that seems to matter.

Melpomene One of the nine Muses: she was the Muse of song,
harmony, but especially tragedy.
'For what ... take her' See Deuteronomy, 20, 7.
Rubric The directions in a Prayer Book.
vitty Fitting (dialect).
house of Atreus The royal house of Argos. Aeschylus, in *Oresteia*,
wrote about its tragic destiny.
house of Jeroboam See 1 Kings, 12: this king of Israel and his
house were cursed by God for setting up images of other gods.
'Royal-tower'd Thame' This comes at the end of John Milton's
At a Vacation Exercise.
shapes like ... multiplied From P. B. Shelley's *The Revolt of
Islam*.
sakes if tidden Heaven's sake if it isn't (dialect).
dibs Children's game, played by throwing up small bones (of a
sheep's leg) or stones.

Chapter 5

The little family of Jude, Sue and Little Father Time settle
down, and early June finds them strolling among the exhibits,
stalls and crowds at Stoke-Barehills on the popular day of
the Great Wessex Agricultural Show. Also present, just from
the London train, are Arabella and her husband Cartlett,
now the landlord of a South London tavern. Arabella recognizes Jude, Sue and her own child (her husband believes him
still to be in Australia). Jude and Sue look happy – so happy

that Arabella suspects they are not married. She then meets Anny, her girlhood friend, and they exchange gossip. There, also, is the so-called 'doctor', Vilbert. Among the exhibits is a model by Jude and Sue. The two groups walk around, Arabella watching the others very closely; the quack sells her a love-philtre, and she and her husband leave for home. Meanwhile, Sue and Jude have enjoyed their day's outing: only the child has remained disinterested and without animation – he betrays a sombre, pessimistic cast of mind.

anxious beings Reminiscent of the lines in Gray's 'Elegy' 'for who, to dumb Forgetfulness a prey/This pleasing anxious being e'er resign'd . . .'

Stoke-Barchills Hardy's name for Basingstoke, Hampshire town. Although it has been steadily industrialized, it still retains many of the features mentioned, except for the site of the 'Great Wessex Show', which was Hardy's name for the Royal Counties Show.

Wintoncester Hardy's name for Winchester. See Note in Part 4, Chapter 4.

Quartershot Hardy's name for Aldershot, in Hampshire, an important military centre.

scot-and-lot freeholder A pre-1832 qualification for voting in borough elections.

Lambeth Borough of S. London, opposite Westminster: Hardy's description which follows was probably apt.

a tale that is told See Psalm 90, 9.

Chapter 6

The young couple's unmarried state causes local gossip and unpleasant remarks at Little Time's school: so they go off quietly to marry, Sue adopting the name of Mrs Fawley. The edge of gossip and scandal is dulled, but the surrounding atmosphere remains unpleasant. Jude in consequence wants to move off elsewhere, but a job turns up at that moment, that of re-lettering the Ten Commandments at a nearby church.

Sue helps him by painting in the letters. Their pleasant work is disturbed by Time's coming from school, crying over some boys' taunts about his mother: a church-cleaner recognizes Sue, their relationship becomes a matter of further gossip and rumour, and Jude loses the job, and even his place at a local workers' society. All this reinforces his intention to move on. They decide to auction off what furniture they have: Jude goes off to secure a lodging. So many places seem barred to them, although they have wronged no one, have always tried to do what they thought was right; yet they remain conspicuous for their apparent resistance to the conventions and restrictions of the time.

Gaymead This is usually considered to be Hardy's name for the village of Theale: it is more likely to be Sulhampstead or Sulhampstead Abbots, about three miles south of Theale.

mind Remember (dialect).

Pugin A. W. N. Pugin (1812–52), a pioneer of the Gothic revival in architecture. He provided the detailed drawings of the Houses of Parliament and designed many Roman Catholic churches.

'we have ... no man!' See 2 Corinthians, 7, 2.

'done that ... own eyes' See Judges, 17, 6.

Chapter 7

Two and a half years pass: the life of the family has been for most of this time almost nomadic, dependent upon wherever Jude has been able to find work. At the spring fair in May at Kennetbridge, the newly widowed Arabella meets Sue, who is tending a confectionery stall with an old-faced boy: Little Father Time. Sue now has two children (apart from Time) and is pregnant. Jude has been ill, so Sue is helping out by selling Christminster cakes, confections decorated with designs representing the colleges and other features of the town. Arabella is now living at Alfredston with her friend

Anny: Sue will not say where she is living, though the shrewd Arabella guesses it is at Kennetbridge. Arabella is going off to a chapel-consecration.

ashlaring Giving a stone facing, or façade, to a wall.

Sandbourne Hardy's name for Bournemouth, a popular Hampshire resort with excellent sands.

Casterbridge Hardy's name for Dorchester, which figures largely in many novels, especially in *The Mayor of Casterbridge*. Many still-existing sites in the town can be positively identified from Hardy's works. His own house, Max Gate, still stands; and the Hardy Memorial dominates the main crossroads in the centre of town.

Exonbury Hardy's name for Exeter, in Devon: a former Roman city on the River Exe: there is a fine cathedral, and many historic sites.

standing Stall.

Chapter 8

Arabella talks to her old friend Anny about Sue and Jude: as they pass the tiny house in which she and Jude first lived, where the pig was killed, she violently expresses the view that Jude belongs more to her than to Sue. Further along the way, they meet, and give a lift to, an elderly man who turns out to be the schoolmaster Mr Phillotson. Arabella recognizes him at once; in mentioning Sue and Jude, the story about the divorce comes out. The master is now reduced in circumstances, mainly because of the scandal surrounding his marriage and separation; yet he is content enough in his own way, though saddened by all the unexpected cruelty of life and nature.

Sue, meanwhile, having sold all her cakes, moves off with the boy, meeting Mrs Edlin – who is helping out at the moment – with her other children: they move on to their cottage. Jude is pale and thin, and is upset at Arabella's further intrusion and proximity. He feels, once again, that the family should move off, this time to his beloved Christminster. Three weeks later they arrive there.

Cresscombe Hardy's name for Letcombe Bassett, a valley village once notable for its watercress beds.
chaw high Be above, scorn the commonplace (dialect).
'Then shall ... iniquity.' See Numbers, 5, 31.

Part 6

Part-title page

'... And she ... torn hair' From Esther, 14, 2.
'There are ... here' From Browning's poem 'Too Late'.

Chapter 1

The family arrives on Christminster's Remembrance Day –
for so Jude had intended – and mingles with the holiday
crowds. Instead of securing lodgings at once, Jude and his
family watch the colourful procession of learned and civic
dignitaries. He is recognized by some of the locals; he talks
to them openly of his gullibility, and the misfortunes – personal and general – that have brought him down. It rains
heavily, but Jude persists in watching the procession to the
end. Sue is distressed at having seen Phillotson among the
crowd. They eventually find lodgings, but not for all the
family – Jude must go elsewhere. Sue is only allowed to stay
overnight, as the landlady's husband will not accept an unmarried woman with children; Sue goes out to try to find
another place, and Little Time morbidly questions why he has
been born at all into such a hostile world.

Remembrance Day This is Hardy's name for the
   Commemoration or Encaenia procession, the annual
   commemoration of founders and benefactors, held at Oxford in
   June.
Italian porch The church of St Mary-the-Virgin.
Lycaonians See Acts, 14, 5–12.
'For who ... under the sun?' From Ecclesiastes, 6, 12.
object glass Lens in a telescope.
um* or *ibus Typical Latin word-endings.

Chapter 2

The lodgings are meagre, cheerless and bare. Little Father Time is anxious and troubled, and questions Sue about the trials and worries of life. He learns, too, that Sue is soon to have another child; he thinks that this will cause extreme distress to all of them and he blames her bitterly – he says that he will never forgive her or ever believe that she really cares for him, for his father or for the rest of the family. Early next morning, Sue, perturbed, goes over to Jude's lodgings to tell him of the situation. After a quick breakfast they return to her lodgings, to find that the children are dead; Time has hanged them, and then himself, because, in his own words, 'we are too menny'. Sue and Jude are frantically distressed and agonized at this desperate, heart-rending event. The inquest and funeral follow: Sue breaks down in her bitter sorrow, and her baby is prematurely stillborn.

Sarcophagus College A sarcophagus is a stone coffin: thus Hardy's reference is naturally (and intentionally) vague. It could be All Souls that is referred to.

Rubric College Not identifiable: Hardy himself thought he might have meant Brasenose College.

universal wish not to live This is an echo of the German philosopher, Arthur Schopenhauer (1788–1860). He asserted that the will is a thing in itself, a compelling force, which manifests itself in the will to live, and which thus in some way maintains the world: once this will to live is abandoned, the world itself must decline.

the eastward position In celebrating the Sacraments, the priest stands facing the east, i.e. towards the Holy Land, with his back to the congregation.

chorus of the Agamemnon From Aeschylus's *Agamemnon*, lines 67–8.

swage Assuage (dialect).

Chapter 3

Sue and Jude move their lodgings: she recovers slowly; Jude finds some work. Sue believes that same fateful goddess of vengeance is pursuing them because of their non-conformity to accepted ritual and convention: Jude believes it to be more a battle against man and human circumstance. Again, they think of the formality of marriage: she wants to remove, somehow, all her past errors and trespasses – and it transpires that she has been attending church services; in a curious way, she feels that she still properly belongs to Phillotson. Arabella visits them: she knows of the tragedy, but not the fact that they remain unmarried. Her father has returned from Australia (her mother having died) and she intends to live with him at Alfredston. Sue, who had gone out, is found by Jude prostrate and sobbing in a church. More than ever now she feels that each is truly married, by sacrament, to another. She wishes only that they could dissolve their bonds, free one another, and live apart, knowing one another as friends perhaps, and possibly in love but not lovers: it is a matter of conscience.

First Cause God, the 'Prime Mover'.

'We are made ... men!' See 1 Corinthians, 4, 9.

sensitive plant The genus of the Mimosa and other plants which close their leaves at the least touch.

chiel ... them ... young man is in their midst Jude is here referring to Robert Burns's poem, 'On the Late Captain Grose's Peregrinations Thro' Scotland': A chiel's amang you takin' notes/And, faith, he'll prent it.

dys Doubtless dysentery, an infection of the colon, and very weakening.

Then let ... hour! The reference is to Mark 15, 38. At the moment of Christ's death, 'the veil of the temple was rent in twain from the top to the bottom'.

Chapter 4

Phillotson now lives at Marygreen: he had seen Sue and Jude during the Christminster festival. He tells his friend Gillingham that he has been thinking about her, and later he reads about her children's tragic death: he meditates even more now. He meets Arabella, who tells him that Sue and Jude have parted, not having after all been married; that Sue has become religious and believes in the binding sarcrament of her marriage to him (Phillotson). Arabella gives him the couple's address. Phillotson feels that, though he has suffered personally and professionally because of Sue and her ways, he would take her back if she were to return willingly. His personal standing and future could only be improved by this. So he writes to her, suggesting that she may return. When Sue tells Jude about the letter, he is bitter, even more so when she suggests that now he can return to Arabella. He believes the whole idea to be wrong-headed and confused; that it will not solve anything. Nevertheless, they part.

volte-face turning-round: sudden and complete change in opinion or in views expressed.

Rhadamanthine strictness In Greek mythology, Rhadamanthus, one of hell's three judges, was rigorously severe but just.

Acherontic shades In Greek mythology the souls (or shades) of the dead crossed the River Acheron into Hades.

'the world ... worth' From Browning's 'The Statue and the Bust'.

'Charity ... her own.' From 1 Corinthians 13, 5.

Chapter 5

Sue goes off to Alfredston that Friday evening. Phillotson is prepared to forgive her completely. Although she finds him physically repellant, Sue wants to go through the remarriage ceremony. Meanwhile, she will stay at the widow Edlin's place, and Gillingham is to come to help out. As a gesture of finality, Sue tears up her attractive nightgown and burns the pieces. The widow-woman thinks ill of Sue's return to Phillotson who, it seems, might now be much more severe and strict with his wife than hitherto. The service is performed: they are rejoined in the sight of God, and Phillotson tells his wife that he does not wish to intrude on her personal privacy.

steam-tram After horse-drawn trams (vehicles moving along rails in urban centres) steam traction was introduced on some lines after 1879, soon giving way to electrification. The one used here was called the Grantham Car, the first of its kind in England.

The Bear The Bear Hotel, still identifiable, in Wantage (Hardy's Alfredston). The frontage retains a period flavour.

night-rails Nightgowns (dialect).

connoted 'Susanna', a form of 'Susan', is derived from a Hebrew word meaning 'lily'.

'Saved as by fire' See 1 Corinthians, 3, 15.

Chapter 6

In the evening of the day on which Sue remarries Phillotson, Arabella, in the drab outskirts of Christminster, is to be found explaining to Jude how she (Arabella) has been turned out destitute from her father's house and has nowhere to go. Eventually she is taken in, and lodges in an attic. Arabella goes to Alfredston to collect some of her things, and returns with the news of Sue's marriage. Arabella plans to 're-capture' Jude if she can: she finds him in a tavern, plies him with drink, and they go back to her father's place (by previous arrangement). Jude is drunk, and babbles a farrago of Biblical, classical, and theological quotations. In the house, in the dark, the fuddled Jude is led upstairs to bed.

templates Mould or pattern shaped to the required outline from which workman execute the shaping of stone, metal, etc.

Holy State By Thomas Fuller (1608–61), English author and clergyman: His *History of the Holy War* appeared in 1639, and three years later *The Holy State and the Profane State*.

'Though I . . . nothing.' Part of the celebrated quotation from 1 Corinthians, 13, 3.

Chapter 7

Arabella's rooms are above her father's little pork shop, just started in business. She tells Mr Donn about Jude, lying upstairs, not yet fully sober, and suffering physically and mentally from drunkenness and the loss of Sue. Arabella has Jude's few belongings brought over, and keeps him in a fuddled state. She suggests they have a party with some of his old friends: the cronies have a convivial time, drinking and playing cards. At a certain point, when Jude is thoroughly confused, Arabella – having arranged all this in advance – takes him off to church, and marries him. Thus is Jude reunited with his first (and strictly, of course, his only) wife.

Capharnaum One of the towns wherein Christ did much of his preaching: see Matthew, 13–16. (Hardy uses here the Aramaic spelling of Capernaum.)

W— of Babylon The whores of Babylon (Revelation, 17–19) – meaning Rome, also worldly luxury and vice.

Chapter 8

Jude and Arabella are in lodgings now, and he is ill, constantly coughing. He asks her to write to Sue whom he still loves: he wants to see her, thinking that he may not have very long to live. He is angered, despite his physical weakness, by Arabella's contempt – and she pretends to agree to his wishes. But one day she finds him gone: it is pouring with rain,

and he is very ill, but he makes his painful way to Marygreen. There he meets Sue, and tells her all that has happened: her marriage is in name only. The cousins still love
each other, hopelessly and helplessly. And Jude, knowing that
he soon will die, makes his wretched way back, through
scenes of his boyhood and childhood, eventually reaching
Christminster.

Hope ... a crumb A bitter allusion to Holy Communion, with its
wine and wafer.

Chapter 9

Arabella is waiting for him at the station. Jude is now des-
perately ill: he upbraids her for not writing. As they walk,
he seems to sense, once again, the ghosts and shades of
Christminster's past great sons: they seem to be laughing
at him. He tells Arabella that when he is dead – which he
thinks will be soon – she will see his spirit there too. Back at
Marygreen, the widow Edlin is, as usual, helping Sue in the
late evening: Sue does not like, and is not good at, domestic
chores. She has not told Phillotson of Jude's visit; but she
feels that now she must be his wife in more than name only.
The ageing schoolmaster, much less patient now, makes her
swear on the New Testament that she will honour and obey,
and do her full duty as a wife. Though physically repelled
at the very thought, Sue submits. The old widow Mrs Edlin
reflects on how times, and marriage, have changed since her
day.

Addison (1672–1719). Famous English essayist and statesman.
Gibbon See Note, p.78.
Johnson The great lexicographer and writer (1709–84) studied at
Pembroke College, Oxford.
Dr Browne Author and physician (1605–82), educated at
Pembroke College (then known as Broadgates Hall), Oxford: his

most celebrated among several learned yet stylish works was
Religio Medici.

Bishop Ken See Note, p.78.

The Poet of Liberty P. B. Shelley (1792–1822). He entered
University College, Oxford in 1810, but was sent down
('rusticated' or expelled) for having collaborated in producing a
pamphlet on *The Necessity of Atheism.* A great deal of his life was
spent in encouraging revolutionary and 'liberating' movements,
a fact strongly reflected in much of his poetry.

Dissector of Melancholy Robert Burton (1577–1640), English
humanist and writer, famous principally for his *The Anatomy of
Melancholy.* He was a student of Brasenose College, Oxford, and in
1599 moved to Christ Church, where he spent the remainder of
his life.

Walter Raleigh Courtier, soldier, explorer, founder of colonies,
poet and author (1552–1618), one of the great Elizabethans,
studied at Oriel College, Oxford.

Wycliffe John Wycliffe (about 1324–84) scholar and reformer,
eventually branded as a heretic for challenging many claims of
the papacy; became Master of Balliol College.

Harvey Neither Gabriel Harvey, the poet and critic, nor William
Harvey, the physician and discoverer of the circulation of the
blood (both born in the middle to late sixteenth century) went to
Oxford.

Hooker Richard Hooker (1554–1600) English theologian, taking
his degree at Corpus Christi, Oxford, wrote the *Laws of
Ecclesiastical Polity.*

Arnold See Note, p.78.

Tractarian shades The 'souls' of the Tractarians, for which see
Note, p.78.

Rubric Jude is here recalling some of the Colleges: Rubric,
possibly Brasenose; Sarcophagus, perhaps All Souls; Crozier,
possibly Oriel or Merton; Tudor – unclear; Cardinal, Christ
Church. Hardy in fact denied that his Christminster was to be
wholly identified with Oxford.

Antigone From Sophocles' *Antigone*, line 851.

un-ray Undress (dialect).

jumps A kind of under-bodice.

Chapter 10

Jude works for a while; then his health breaks down again. He and Arabella are quite indifferent to each other. He often rambles on about his past life and its failures; how he was fated to obscurity and wretchedness. Unexpectedly, Mrs Edlin calls and tells him about Sue's voluntary submission to Phillotson: this distresses Jude acutely. Arabella has called the doctor, the quack Vilbert, but Jude dismisses him sharply. But Arabella treats Vilbert to a drink, with his own love-philtre in it, and they kiss. For Arabella, the quack physician is in reserve, as she says, 'for a rainy day', as she cannot expect Jude to survive very long now.

benzoline A light hydrocarbon derived from petroleum, formerly used in lamps.

Chapter 11

Summer comes round: Jude is thin and weak. Arabella is preparing to go out to enjoy herself in the pleasant open air. It is again Remembrance Day, the festival of Christminster. Jude hears and recognizes the distant sounds, so full of memories. In his weak, feverish state he calls for water but there is no one to respond. Reciting at length a tragic passage from the Book of Job, he dies. Meanwhile Arabella, flaunting herself, has been asked to join a happy group going down river to watch the sports. Returning, she finds Jude dead: she leaves, nevertheless, saying that he is asleep. She joins in the fun, and meets Vilbert. Eventually she goes back, and Jude's body is laid out for burial. Two days later, Arabella and the widow Edlin look for the last time at Jude's face in his open coffin. We learn that Sue is miserably unhappy with Phillotson, and Arabella feels that Sue will never find real peace until, like her cousin Jude, she too dies.

Oldgate College New College, Oxford.
'Let the day ... Bitter in soul?' From Job, 3, 3–20.
Cardinal Street Hardy's name for St Aldate's Street: the lodging
  in which Jude died remains elusive and probably, being fictitious,
  undiscoverable.

Revision questions

Part 1

1 Summarize the important facts of Jude's life up to the age of nineteen.

2 Why has Jude set his heart on studying at Christminster?

3 Give an account of Jude's first encounter with Arabella. Why does he eventually marry her?

4 Describe the scene of the pig-killing. What new characteristics of Jude and Arabella does it reveal?

5 From the point of view of each member of the married couple, show how the marriage of Jude and Arabella results in miserable failure.

6 What part is played in this section by: a) Mr Phillotson; b) Drusilla Fawley; c) 'Doctor' Vilbert?

Part 2

1 Describe the appearance and attitude to life of Jude when first he lodges in Christminster.

2 State the various circumstances by which Jude eventually meets his cousin Sue Bridehead.

3 Why was Sue forced to leave her lodgings?

4 What new information about the Fawley family is provided by Jude's great-aunt?

5 What effect did the College Master's letter have upon Jude? In your opinion, is the letter justified in its contents?

6 Why does Jude return to Marygreen?

Part 3

1 How does Jude set about his new resolve?

2 What is Sue's opinion of conventional, organized religion as so far expressed by her in this section of the novel?

3 Why did Sue run away from the Training-school?

4 Give a careful account of Sue's background as revealed in this Part.

5 How does Phillotson begin to feature more strongly in these chapters? What does he now think of Sue? Why does she express a wish to marry him?

6 Explain the circumstances in which Arabella is re-introduced into the story. What does she now think of Jude, and he of her?

7 What is the point of the hymn-composer episode?

Part 4

1 What is the opinion of both Jude and Sue to her marriage to Phillotson? What does the schoolmaster think of his wife?

2 Why is Mr Gillingham introduced into the story at this point?

3 Why does Sue return to Jude?

4 What happens to Phillotson as a consequence of Sue's departure?

Part 5

1 Why cannot Jude and Sue decide upon marriage?

2 What effect has Arabella's re-appearance: a) on Sue; b) on Jude? What now does each think of the other?

3 Why do Sue and Jude agree to take over the welfare and upkeep of Arabella's child? Why does not Arabella herself continue to look after him?

4 Describe the appearance and character of Little Father Time.

5 Give an account of every significant point relating to the attitudes to one another of the principal characters, as seen at the Great Wessex Agricultural Show.

6 Why eventually do Jude and Sue have to leave Aldbrickham? In what circumstances does Arabella again intervene in their lives?

7 What has happened to Phillotson meanwhile? Show how he is again interwoven into the story.

Part 6

1 Why did Jude return to Christminster on Remembrance Day?

2 What are the essential points of Jude's 'speech' to the crowd? What changes in his previous thinking are revealed in it?

3 Give an account of Little Father Time's quarrel with Sue (Chapter 2). How and why does this lead to the deaths of the children?

4 What are the separate reactions of Sue and Jude, after the initial shock, to the tragedy of the children's deaths?

5 What effect has Arabella's visit upon Sue; and the news of the children's deaths upon Phillotson?

6 Why does Sue return to Phillotson? What arrangement about their marriage do they agree to?

7 How and why does Arabella renew her closer acquaintance with Jude?

8 Describe the situation surrounding the episode of Jude's death.

General questions

1 Summarize the plot of *Jude the Obscure* within twenty to thirty lines.

2 Trace the 'vision' of Christminster in Jude's life, from its origins to its extinction.

3 Compare and contrast Jude's concept of Christminster with the reality.

4 What were the principal factors underlying Jude's 'conversion'?

5 Do you find Jude always a tragic figure? Give instances where he is treated with another emphasis.

6 In what ways is Sue Bridehead to be considered a 'modern' woman?

7 Why did Sue marry Mr Phillotson?

8 Write a defence of Arabella Donn.

9 In your own words, reconstruct the episode of Jude's death as seen through the eyes of Arabella.

10 What is the overall attitude of a) Sue and b) Arabella, towards Jude: how do they view him; and do their attitudes towards him change through their contact with him?

11 A critic has commented, 'Arabella lives.' What do you think he wished to suggest or convey by this?

12 What would the novel have gained, or lost, without the roles played by a) Drusilla Fawley, and b) Mrs Edlin?

13 What positive, favourable qualities have you found in Mr Phillotson?

14 Write brief notes on the roles and characters of a) 'Physician' Vilbert, and b) Mr Gillingham.

15 Little Father Time has been called the 'worst failure' of the novel. Do you agree? What do you make of him?

16 Apart from the deaths of the children, which scene of the book have you found the most striking? Why?

17 Show how Part 4: At Shaston marks a turning-point in the whole movement of the novel.

18 Hardy, according to one critic, was 'not a great craftsman'. Discuss this in view of the structure and style of this novel.

19 How far, in your opinion, does coincidence affect the mainstream of the story?

20 Do you regard the novel as 'a failed tragedy'?